Volume 17

make it yourself

The Complete Step-by-Step Library of Needlework and Crafts

COLUMBIA HOUSE/New York

Editor: Mary Harding
Assistant Editor: Margo Coughtrie
Editorial Assistants: Sally Fisher/Maureen Paton
Consultants: Greta Barrett/Angela Jeffs (Sewing)/
Patsy North (Embroidery and Crafts)/
Frances Rogers (Knitting and Crochet)
Managing Editor: Nicholas Wright
Design Co-ordinator: Jan Churcher
Production Control: Sheila Biddlecombe
Editorial Director: Graham Donaldson

Distributed by Columbia House, 51 West 52nd Street, New York, New York 10019

Printed in U.S.A.

Introduction

More advanced knitters will have plenty to get their needles into in Volume 17 of Make It Yourself. You can create beautifully-patterned pullovers and cardigans by using yarn in several colors and following the designs on a chart. As well as the wide selection of patterns for you and the children, there are knitted pillow covers which you will be proud to display in your home.

Crochet goes lacy with a bikini set for the beach, a delicate yoke for a blouse, a pair of feminine gloves, and lots more. Again, there is plenty which those who are experienced with a crochet hook will find an absorbing challenge.

If you feel like a sporty summer, deck yourself out from our dressmaking section. Jackets, pants, over-alls, cotton dresses—you'll find something to suit you. You can also learn how to set in a sleeve gusset and make a pleated skirt on a yoke.

For embroidery addicts, we give a choice of cool embroidered blouses as well as ideas for satin stitch in needlepoint. Learn also how decorative and useful quilting is in the home.

Children love to be outdoors in the summer, so why not make them a play tent or a special hammock. Even baby is not forgotten—he has his own special basket for summer walks.

make it yourself

Contents   Page

How to use this book...

Selecting a yarn

In this series, we are introducing a new and easy way to identify the yarn used in our knitting and crochet features! You will find an actual-size, colored photograph of the yarn given with each set of directions.

Materials Required:

150 (200) gm or 6 (7) oz each of yellow and green, 50gm or 2oz blue [100 gm = 360m or 390yds]. Knitting needles size 4 (Am) or 10 (Eng).

At one time or another, you have probably suffered the disappointment of finding that the yarn specified in knitting and crochet directions is difficult to obtain or totally unavailable in your area. When this happens you are faced with the often impossible task of finding a substitute yarn. By matching a yarn against our photograph, you can choose a yarn of similar weight and texture from the range of yarns available in your store or favorite needlework shop.

This method is also helpful if you have yarn left over from other projects and you are unsure whether it is the proper weight or texture and whether you have sufficient yardage to finish a new shawl or pullover.

To help you determine the amount of yarn needed, we have also listed the yardage per skein for the yarn used. Most yarn companies give the yardage per skein in their sample books, and many shops have interchangeable yarn lists which give the yardages per unit weight. You will then be able to see whether you will need to make adjustments in the number of skeins required of the yarn which you have chosen.

Before you start to work the pattern, work a test swatch and match it against the Tension given in the directions (see the Tension Gauge instructions below). Adjust the needle or hook size if necessary. Any yarn which can be worked at the tension given in the directions can be used for that pattern.

Centimeters or inches?

The metric system of measurement is gaining greater use and acceptance, and some needlework and crafts equipment and materials are already sold by the metric weight and/or length. For your convenience, we have given all the weights and measures in both systems. NOTE: In some cases, the conversions are not exact. The measurements have been rounded to the nearest convenient or appropriate number.

Tension gauge

One key to successful knitting or crocheting is the tension! Each of our directions is based on the given tension gauge (number of rows and stitches to 10cm or 4"). To check your tension, work a test piece 12cm or 5" square in the stitch pattern. Make a cardboard template with a 10cm or 4" square cut out of it. Place the template over your swatch and count the rows and stitches. Compare the numbers with the tension gauge given in the directions. If your swatch has too few stitches and rows, work more tightly or use smaller equipment. If you have more than the number given, use larger needles, or hook.

Directions for the items shown can be used for any yarn of similar thickness and texture, providing you can achieve the proper tension.

Do not be upset if you find that you do have to adjust the needle or hook size. This does not mean that there is anything wrong with your knitting or crocheting. The needle and hook sizes given in the directions are an average, but by no means an absolute. There is great variation in the tension at which different people work, and you will even find slight variations in the tension of your work. On days when you are tense or tired, your knitting or crocheting will probably be a little tighter.

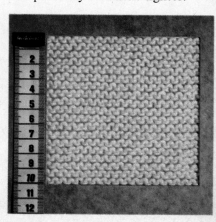

Fashion sizing

Dressmaking

Do you know your size? Don't just say 'yes', because as you already know, the fit of pattern and ready-to-wear sizes varies.

To eliminate confusion, we have lettered our sizes (A, B, C) instead of giving them the traditional numbering (10, 12).

Remeasure yourself and match your body measurements with those given in the chart below. All of the patterns are designed according to these measurements, so choose the pattern size which is right for your measurements. You may have to make minor adjustments in the pattern pieces to adapt them to your body contours, and Dressmaking Pattern Sheet 2 explains how to do this. Other dressmaking pattern sheets will deal with more complex fitting for specific garments such as pants.

DO NOT MEASURE THE PATTERNS. Every pattern includes, according to the design, an added measure to allow for easy movement when wearing the garment. Just compare your body measurements with the measurements given in the chart and choose the proper size.

Each pattern is given in five sizes. Two of the sizes are given on the pattern sheet and the other three sizes can be easily drawn from the two sizes given. Directions for adapting for the three additional sizes are given on each pattern sheet. Even if you are not one of the standard pattern sizes, but are a mixed size made up of several standard measurements, you can still use our patterns. Since each pattern can be adapted for five sizes – a size smaller, a size larger, and a size between the two sizes actually marked on the pattern sheet – it is possible to construct a pattern for yourself. Directions for constructing a mixed-size pattern are given on Dressmaking Pattern Sheet 2.

Knitting and Crochet

The knitting and crochet sizes are based on the Dressmaking Body Measurements Chart. For each direction, you will be given the actual body measurements for which the garment is intended. The finished knitted or crocheted garment will be larger than the given measurements to allow for comfort and movement.

Size: Directions are for 92 cm (36″) bust. Changes for 96, 100 cm (37½″, 39½″) bust are in brackets.

Do you know your size?

Don't just say 'yes'. Remeasure yourself, following the diagrams and instructions, and then check the Body Measurements chart.

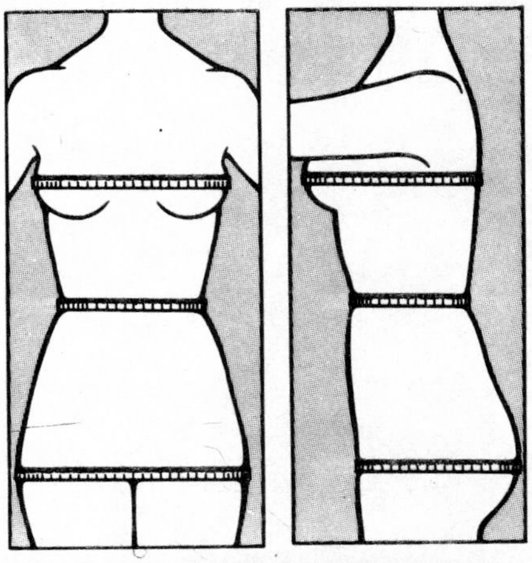

Bust – measure around the fullest part of the bust.

Waist – tie a string around your body so that it settles comfortably at your natural waistline. Measure your waist at the string.

Hips – measure around the fullest part of your hips (this generally falls 7″–9″ below your waistline).

Important hints:

When taking measurements, do not hold the tape measure slack or pull it too tight. The tape must lie evenly horizontal all around the body – it should not go up at the back and down at the front. You will find it simpler and more accurate to be measured by someone else.

Body measurements chart

WOMEN

Size	A	B	C	D	E	F	G	H
Bust	80 cm (31½″)	84 cm (33″)	88 cm (34½″)	92 cm (36″)	96 cm (37½″)	100 cm (39½″)	104 cm (41″)	108 cm (42½″)
Waist	59 cm (23¼″)	63.5 cm (25″)	68 cm (26½″)	72.5 cm (28½″)	77 cm (30½″)	81.5 cm (32″)	86 cm (34″)	90 cm (35½″)
Hips	86 cm (34″)	90 cm (35½″)	94 cm (37″)	98 cm (38½″)	102 cm (40″)	106 cm (42″)	110 cm (43½″)	114 cm (45″)

MEN

Size	J	K	L	M	N	O	P	Q
Chest	84 cm (33″)	88 cm (34½″)	92 cm (36″)	96 cm (37½″)	100 cm (39½″)	104 cm (41″)	108 cm (42½″)	112 cm (44″)
Hip	88 cm (34½″)	92 cm (36″)	96 cm (37½″)	100 cm (39½″)	104 cm (41″)	108 cm (42½″)	112 cm (44″)	116 cm (45½″)
Neck	36 cm (14″)	37 cm (14½″)	38 cm (15″)	39 cm (15½″)	40 cm (15¾″)	41 cm (16″)	42 cm (16½″)	43 cm (17″)
Arm	60 cm (23¾″)	61 cm (24″)	62 cm (24¼″)	63 cm (24¾″)	64 cm (25¼″)	65 cm (25½″)	66 cm (26″)	67 cm (26½″)

CHILDREN

Size	S	T	U	V	W	X	Y	Z
Height	110 cm (43″)	116 cm (45½″)	122 cm (48″)	128 cm (50½″)	134 cm (52¾″)	140 cm (55″)	146 cm (57½″)	152 cm (60″)
Chest	60 cm (23¾″)	62 cm (24¼″)	64 cm (25¼″)	66 cm (26″)	68 cm (26¾″)	70 cm (27½″)	73 cm (28¾″)	76 cm (29¾″)
Waist	58 cm (23″)	59 cm (23¼″)	60 cm (23¾″)	61 cm (24″)	62 cm (24¼″)	63 cm (24¾″)	64 cm (25¼″)	65 cm (25¾″)
Hips	66 cm (26″)	68 cm (26¾″)	70 cm (27½″)	72 cm (28¼″)	74 cm (29″)	76 cm (29¾″)	80 cm (31½″)	84 cm (33″)

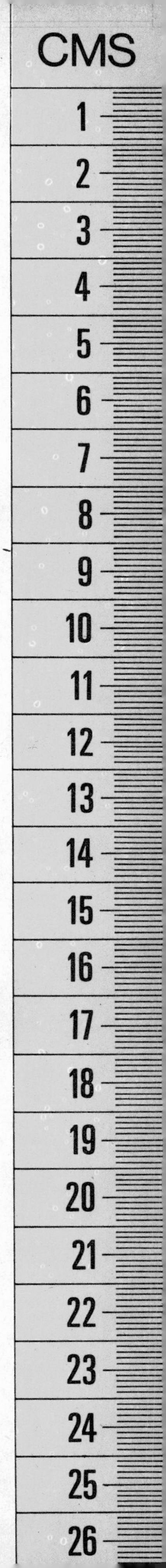
CMS
1
2
3
4
5
6
7
8
9
10
11
12
13
14
15
16
17
18
19
20
21
22
23
24
25
26

In the best tradition

The two cardigans shown here and overleaf combine fine knitting with traditional patterning. Neither is for the complete beginner as both patience and skill are required.

Size: Directions are for 84 cm or 33" bust. Changes for 92 cm or 36" bust are in brackets.

Materials Required:

[100 gm = 240 m or 262 yds]. Cardigan 1: 120 (150) gm or 5 (6) oz light blue, 90 gm or 4 oz each of dark blue and white. Cardigan 2: 240 (270) gm or 9 (10) oz red, 60 gm or 3 oz light green, 30 gm or 2 oz each of dark green and white. Knitting needles and circular needle size 2 (Am) or 11 (Eng). 5 buttons.

Basic Stitch: St st.

Cardigan 1: Color Sequence: *2 R dark blue, 2 R white, and 2 R light blue, repeat from *.

Knitting Chart: Repeat R 1–37 1 time, repeating the 12 sts across R. Each x represents 1 st in corresponding color, except grey which represents white.

Cardigan 2: Knitting Chart: Repeat R 1–93 for Back and

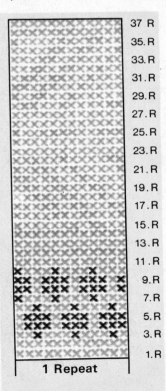

	37 R
	35 R
	33 R
	31 R
	29 R
	27 R
	25 R
	23 R
	21 R
	19 R
	17 R
	15 R
	13 R
	11 R
	9 R
	7 R
	5 R
	3 R
	1 R

1 Repeat

Knitting Chart: Each X = 1 st in that color except grey which = white.

2059

Front; the beginning and end are given in instructions. Each x represents 1 st in corresponding color, except grey which represents white. Use a circular needle and work back and forth. For single R stripes, begin where color hangs at the side. This means that some R will be 2 right side R then 2 wrong side R.

Tension: 24 sts and 38 R = 10 cm or 4″.

Abbreviations: K = knit. P = purl. St(s) = stitch(es). R = row(s). St st = stocking or stockinette stitch.

DIRECTIONS

Back (for both designs): Using main color, cast on 100 (110) sts and work 10 cm or 4″ in K 1, P 1 rib. Change to Basic Stitch and Color Sequence for Cardigan 1 or work from Knitting Chart for Cardigan 2 to 30 cm or 11¾″.

Shape Armholes: At beginning of every R, cast off 3 sts 4 (6) times, 2 sts 4 times, 3 sts 2 times, and 1 st at each end of following 4th R − 72 (76) sts. Work straight to 47 (48) cm or 18½″ (19″).

Shape Neck and Shoulders: Cast off center 28 sts and work on each side separately. At neck edge, in every 2nd R cast off 2 sts 2 times and 1 st 1 time. *At the same time,* at armhole edge, in every 2nd R cast off 4 sts 3 (1) time(s) and 5 sts 1 (3) time(s).

Left Front: Using main color, cast on 48 (53) sts and work 10 cm or 4″ in K 1, P 1 rib. Change to st st and shape armhole and shoulder as for Back. Cardigan 1: Work in Color Sequence to 28 cm or 11″, then decrease 1 st at front edge on next R and every 3rd R 7 times, every 4th R 5 times, then every 6th R 4 times. *At the same time,* work from the Knitting Chart for 37 R, then in Color Sequence, beginning with a wrong side R. Cardigan 2:

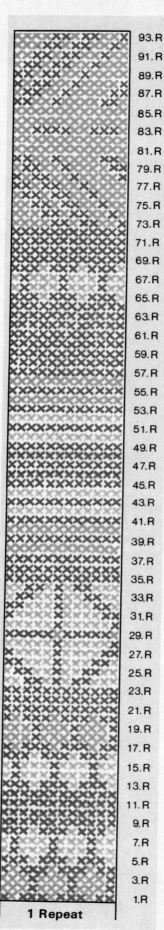

93.R
91.R
89.R
87.R
85.R
83.R
81.R
79.R
77.R
75.R
73.R
71.R
69.R
67.R
65.R
63.R
61.R
59.R
57.R
55.R
53.R
51.R
49.R
47.R
45.R
43.R
41.R
39.R
37.R
35.R
33.R
31.R
29.R
27.R
25.R
23.R
21.R
19.R
17.R
15.R
13.R
11.R
9.R
7.R
5.R
3.R
1.R

1 Repeat

▲ The front of this second cardigan is patterned all over, with only a few narrow stripes on the sleeves to balance the design.

◀ Knitting Chart: Each X = 1 st in that color except grey which = white.

Half-pattern for ▶ small (large) size. The numbers are centimeters; inches are in the directions.

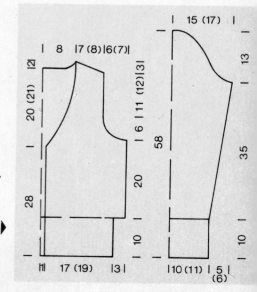

Here, the patterning is shown more clearly. Compare it with the chart when working the design.

Work R 35–60 of Knitting Chart 1 time, beginning 1st R on right edge with sts 8–12 1 time, then sts 1–12 4 times. Then work R 1–93, and again from R 35 until work measures same as Back to shoulder. Work armhole and shoulder as for Back and Front shapings as for Cardigan 1.

Right Front: Work to match Left Front, reversing all shapings, and for Cardigan 2, work 1st R of Knitting Chart from sts 1–12 4 times, then sts 1–5 1 time.

Sleeves: Using main color, cast on 48 (54) sts and work in K 1, P 1 rib for 10 cm or 4″. Continue in st st in Color Sequence for Cardigan 1 and for Cardigan 2 work R 37–56 of Knitting Chart, then work in main color only. *At the same time,* increase 1 st each end of every 10th R (alternately every 8th and 10th R) 12 (14) times — 72 (82) sts. Work straight to 45 cm or 17¾″.

Shape Top: At beginning of every R, cast off 4 (6) sts 2 times, 3 sts 2 times, 2 sts 4 times, 1 st 4 times, then 1 st each end of every 4th R 6 times. Then at beginning of every R, cast off 1 st 4 times, 2 sts 4 times, 3 sts 2 times, 4 (6) sts 2 times — 8 (10) sts. Cast off.

Front Band: Using main color and circular needle, cast on 286 (290) sts and work in st st for 1 cm or ⅜″, ending after a P R. Work buttonholes in next R over 3 sts, placing the 1st one 3 cm or 1¼″ from beginning of R and 4 more at 5 cm or 2″ intervals. In next R cast on 3 sts in place of those cast off. Work another set at 3 cm or 1¼″. Cast off loosely at 4 cm or 1½″.

Finishing: Join all seams. Sew Front Band to Fronts and Back neck edge, fold in half and stitch down. Work buttonhole stitch around double buttonholes. Sew on the buttons. Press.

This attractive design is worked in several colors and alternated with plain stripes. The sleeves and back are in plain navy blue. All the borders are in rib and the neckband is sewn on.

This version of the pullover is basically grey highlighted by bands of patterning in black, green, red, salmon, and white. Like the beige version, it is hip-length with turn-back bands at the V-neck.

FOR BOTH
Materials Required:

Colors and quantities are given in individual directions [50gm = 165 m or 180yds]. Knitting needles sizes 1 and 2 (Am) or 11 and 12 (Eng).

Basic Stitch: St st.

Knitting Pattern 2: See the chart below right. 1 repeat of st pattern and end st are given.

Tension: 28 sts and 39 R = 10cm or 4".

Abbreviations: K = knit. P = purl. St(s) = stitch(es). R = row(s). St st = stocking or stockinette stitch.

MOTHER

Size: Directions are for 84cm or 33" bust. Changes for 92cm or 36" bust are in brackets.

Yarn: 350 (400) gm or 13 (15) oz rust, 100gm or 4oz white, small amounts of dark green, navy, yellow and beige.

Knitting Pattern 1: R 1–6: (R 1 is right side) In rust in st st. R 7: K 1 rust (edge st), K 3 rust, *1 white, 5 rust, repeat from *, ending 3 rust instead of 5, then K 1 rust (edge st). R 8–13: In rust in st st. R 14: K 1 rust (edge st), *1 white, 5 rust, repeat from *, ending 1 white, 1 rust (edge st). Repeat R 1–14.

DIRECTIONS

Back: Using rust and finer needles, cast on 100 (112) sts and work 12 cm or 4¾" in K 1, P 1 rib. Change to thicker needles, white, and st st and increase in next R thus: K 2 (8),

*K 3, increase in next st, repeat from *, ending K 6 (12) – 123 (135) sts. Work 1 R white, then 2 R each of navy, beige, dark green, and white. Change to Knitting Pattern 1 and work straight to 30 (31) cm or 11¾" (12¼").

Shape Armholes: At beginning of every R, cast off 3 sts 2 times, 2 sts 4 times, and 1 st 10 times – 99 (111) sts. Work straight to 39 (41) cm or 15¼" (16¼"), then work 2 R white. Now work the 39 R of Knitting Pattern 2, but keep an edge st each end in main color of R. R 1 will read: K 1 (edge st), repeat 1–6th st 16 (18) times, K end st, then K 1 (edge st). When Knitting Pattern 2 is complete, work 2 R white. Change to finer needles and rust and work 2 cm or ¾" in K 1, P 1 rib. Cast off loosely in rib.

Front: Work as for Back, but begin Knitting Pattern 2 at 35 (37) cm or 13¾" (14½"), then work as given for Back.

Sleeves: Using finer needles and rust, cast on 56 (62) sts and work 3 cm or 1¼" in K 1, P 1 rib. Change to thicker needles, white, and st st and increase in next R thus: (K 1, K twice in next st) 9 (12) times, K twice in next 18 (13) sts, (K 1, K twice in next st) 9 (12) times, K 1 – 93 (99) sts. Work 1 R white, then work the 39 R of Knitting Pattern 2 as for Back. Work 2 R white, then continue straight in Knitting Pattern 1 to 45 cm or 17¾".

Shape Top: At beginning of every R, cast off 3 sts 4 times, 2 sts 10 times, 1 st 12 times, 2 sts 10 times, and 3 sts 4 times – 17 (23) sts. Cast off.

Finishing: Press on wrong side with

a warm iron over a damp cloth. Pin Back shoulders under Front for 4 cm or 1½", then stitch down. Sew in sleeves. Sew up all seams.

DAUGHTER

Size: Directions are for 68cm or 26¾" chest. Changes for 72cm or 28" chest are in brackets.

Yarn: 250 (300) gm or 9 (11) oz dark green, 50gm or 2oz white, small amounts of navy, yellow, rust and beige.

Knitting Pattern 1: See Mother's Pullover, working dark green in place of rust.

DIRECTIONS

Back: Using dark green and finer needles, cast on 84 (90) sts and work 10cm or 4" in K 1, P 1 rib. Change to thicker needles, st st, and white and for small size increase in next R thus: K 6, *increase in next st, K 4. Repeat from * 14 times more, K 3. For larger size, increase in every 6th st. There are now 99 (105) sts. Work 1 R white, then 2 R

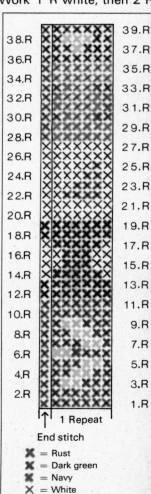

Knitting Pattern 2: 1 repeat of pattern and end stitch are given. Each cross = 1 stitch in that color for Mother; for Daughter, the last 4 rows are rust instead of dark green.

1 Repeat
End stitch

✕ = Rust
✕ = Dark green
✕ = Navy
✕ = White
✕ = Yellow
✕ = Beige

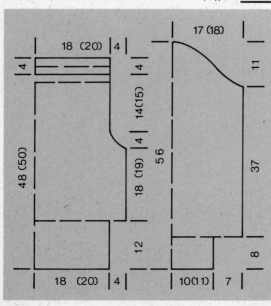

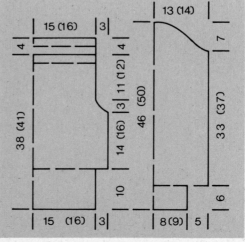

Half-patterns in small (large) sizes for Mother, left, and Daughter, right. The numbers are centimeters; inch equivalents are given in the directions.

For the girls

each of rust, navy, beige, and white. Now work Knitting Pattern 1 to 24 (26) cm or 9½″ (10¼″).

Shape Armholes: At beginning of every R, cast off 2 sts 6 times and 1 st 6 times – 81 (87) sts. Work to 32 (35) cm or 12½″ (13¾″). Work 2 R white, then work from R 12–39 of Knitting Pattern 2 (with edge sts), working the last 4 R in rust instead of dark green. Work 2 more R white. Change to dark green and finer

needles; work 2 cm or ¾″ in K 1, P 1 rib. Cast off in rib.

Front: Work as for Back, but work Knitting Pattern 2 at 28 (31) cm or 11″ (12¼″).

Sleeves: Using dark green and finer needles, cast on 44 (50) sts and work 6 cm or 2½″ in K 1, P 1 rib. Change to thicker needles, st st, and white and increase in next R thus: (K 1, increase in next st) 6 (10) times, increase in next 18 (12) sts, (K

1, increase in next st) 7 (9) times – 75 (81) sts. Work 1 R white. Now work R 12–39 of Knitting Pattern 2, working the last 4 R in rust instead of dark green. Work 2 R white, then in Knitting Pattern 1 to 39 (43) cm or 15¼″ (17″), or length required.

Shape Top: At beginning of every R, cast off 3 sts 4 times, 2 sts 20 times, 3 sts 4 times. Cast off remaining 11 (17) sts.

Finishing: See Mother's Pullover.

Boys will be boys

An unusual colored pattern livens up this pullover for boys.

Size: Directions are for 71 cm or 28″ chest. Changes for 76 cm or 30″ chest are in brackets.

Materials Required:

300 (350) gm or 11 (13) oz brown or rust, 50 gm or 2 oz beige or white, small amount of red or green [100 gm = 360 m or 390 yds]. Knitting needles sizes 1 and 2 (Am) or 11 and 12 (Eng). Circular needle size 1 (Am) or 12 (Eng).

Tension: 23 sts, 36 R = 10 cm or 4″.

Abbreviations: K = knit. P = purl. St st = stocking or stockinette st.

DIRECTIONS

Back: Using finer needles and brown or rust, cast on 84 (92) sts and work 8 cm or 3″ in K 1, P 1 rib. Change to thicker needles and st st; work straight to 32 (34) cm or 12½″ (13½″). At beginning of next 2 R, cast on 7 sts – 98 (106) sts. Now work the 44 (52) R of Knitting Chart, knitting 1 st each end as edge st (not shown on chart). Continue in brown or rust and work to 50 (53) cm or 19¾″ (21″).

Shape Neck and Shoulders: Cast off center 22 sts and work on each side separately. At neck edge, in every 2nd R cast off 2 sts 4 times, 1 st 1 time. *At the same time,* at armhole edge, in every 2nd R cast off 11 (12) sts 2 times, 11 (13) sts 1 time.

Front: As Back to end of pattern.

Shape Neck: Cast off center 10 sts and work on each side separately. At neck edge, in every 2nd R cast off 2 sts 3 times and 1 st 5 times, then work straight to 50 (53) cm or 19¾″ (21″), ending at armhole edge. Shape shoulder as for Back.

Sleeves: Using finer needles and brown or rust, cast on 42 (46) sts and work 8 cm or 3″ in K 1, P 1 rib. Change to thicker needles and work in st st, increasing in every 4th st – 52 (56) sts. Now increase 1 st each end of every 8th R 14 times – 80 (84) sts. *At the same time,* when work measures 29 (31) cm or 11½″ (12¼″), work from Knitting Chart as for Back, placing pattern centrally, then work 2 R brown or rust. Cast off loosely.

Finishing: Press work. Join seams. Using circular needle and brown or rust, pick up and K 92 sts around neck edge. Work in rnds of K 1, P 1 rib for 2.5 cm or 1″. Cast off in rib.

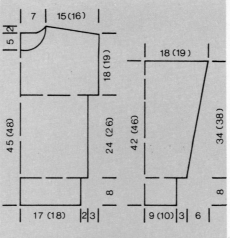
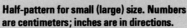
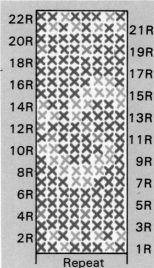

Half-pattern for small (large) size. Numbers are centimeters; inches are in directions.

Knitting Chart: One repeat of the pattern is given. For the smaller size, work R 1–22 2 times. For the larger size, work R 19–22 1 time, R 1–22 2 times, and R 1–4 1 time. For the brown pullover, follow the colors shown. For the rust pullover, substitute rust for brown, white for beige, and green for red.

Repeat

Stars and stripes for ever!

Sizes: Pullover directions are for 56 (60) cm or 22" (23½") chest. Hat directions are for 50 (52) cm or 19¾" (20½") head size.

Materials Required:

Pullover: 50 (100) gm or 2 (4) oz red *or* dark blue. Hat: 50 gm or 2 oz red *or* dark blue. For Both: 50 gm or 2 oz each of white, medium blue, light blue, yellow, green, and red *or* dark blue [100 gm = 400 m or 437 yds]. Knitting needles sizes 1 and 2 (Am)

or 11 and 12 (Eng). Circular needle size 1 (Am) or 12 (Eng). Stitch holder.

Basic Stitch: St st.

Knitting Diagram: 1 repeat of pattern consists of 22 sts and 44 R. The outlined squares are knitted in the main color of the area and later embroidered over in the color shown.

Color Sequence: (for Hat) 2 R each medium blue, white, light blue, green, yellow, 2 R red *or* dark blue.

Tension: 30 sts and 40 R = 10 cm or 4".

Abbreviations: K = knit. P = purl. St(s) = stitch(es). R = row(s). St st = stocking or stockinette stitch.

PULLOVER

Back: Using finer needles and red *or* dark blue, cast on 85 (91) sts and work 4 cm or 1½" in K 1, P 1 rib. Change to thicker needles and st st, repeating 44 R of Knitting Diagram, working 1st R thus: for 1st size, K 1 (edge st) then K sts 4–22 1 time, sts 1–22 2 times, sts 1–20 1 time, K 1 (edge st). For 2nd size, K 1 (edge st) then sts 1–22 4 times, K end st, K 1 (edge st). Continue straight to 32 (37) cm or 12½" (14½").

Shape Neck: Cast off center 21 sts and work on each side separately. At neck edge, in every 2nd R cast off

The bright splashes of color harmonize well in our adventurous design. Use a dominant color for the ribs, such as red and blue as shown here, to give unity to the multi-colored design. The white dots, hearts, and zigzag lines are outlined in Swiss darning or duplicate stitch.

Knitting Diagram is for the red Pullover. For the blue Pullover, with the exception of the red hearts, reverse the red and blue stitches. One cross = one stitch. One repeat of the pattern consists of 22 stitches and 44 rows. The outlined stitches are knitted in the main color of the area and later embroidered in the color shown with Swiss darning or duplicate stitch.

Half-pattern for small (large) size. The numbers are centimeters; inches are in the directions.

Red = ✕
Yellow = ✕
Green = ✕
Light blue = ✕
White = ✕
Dark blue = ✕
Medium blue = ✕

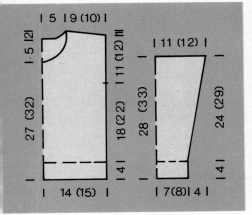

43.R
41.R
39.R
37.R
35 R
33.R
31.R
29.R
27.R
25.R
23.R
21.R
19.R
17.R
15.R
13.R
11.R
9.R
7.R
5.R
3.R
1.R

End stitch   1 Repeat

2 sts 2 times and 1 st 1 time. *At the same time,* at 33 (38) cm or 13" (15") shape shoulders at armhole edge in every 2nd R by casting off 9 (10) sts 3 times.

Front: Work as for Back to 27 (32) cm or 10½" (12½").

Shape Neck: Cast off center 9 sts and work on each side separately. At neck edge, in every 2nd R cast off 2 sts 2 times and 1 st 5 times. At 33 (38) cm or 13" (15"), shape shoulder as for Back.

Sleeves: Using finer needles and red *or* dark blue, cast on 45 (51) sts and work 4 cm or 1½" in K 1, P 1 rib. Change to thicker needles and work in Knitting Diagram, working 1st R thus: for 1st size, K 1 (edge st), K sts 2–22 1 time, sts 1–22 1 time, K 1 (edge st). For 2nd size, K sts 20–22

1 time, sts 1–22 2 times, sts 1–4 1 time.

Continue in pattern as set, increasing 1 st each end of every 8th (10th) R 11 times — 67 (73) sts. Cast off at 28 (33) cm or 11" (13").

Neckband: Using circular needle and red *or* dark blue, cast on 108 sts and work 4 cm or 1½" in K 1, P 1 rib. Cast off in rib.

Finishing: Using Swiss darning or duplicate stitch, embroider over the knitted sts on the red pullover in dark blue along the zigzag lines; embroider the red hearts above the blue stars. On the blue pullover, the zigzag lines are in red and the hearts embroidered in red so that they lie in between the stars. Embroider star centers as shown. Pin out; press. Join seams, sew on Neckband.

HAT

Cast on 145 (149) sts, using finer needles and red *or* dark blue yarn. Work 3 cm or 1¼" in K 1, P 1 rib. Change to thicker needles and st st and work 6 R in white, then 4 cm or 1½" in red *or* dark blue. Reverse work for turn-back by purling next R and work in Color Sequence to 21 cm or 8¼". In next R, K 1 (3), *K 2 together, K 16. Repeat from * to end, ending K 2 for 2nd size. Continue thus, decreasing on every R with 1 st less between decreases each time 15 times more — 17 (21) sts. Break off yarn, draw through. Fasten off.

Finishing: Embroider hearts onto the wide white stripe of the turn-back, then onto the 3rd Color Sequence work zigzag line in dark blue *or* red, beginning at center. Join seam.

2071

Feet first!

Knit colorful house socks with leather soles for the family.

For all styles

Materials Required:

[50 gm = 133 m or 145 yds]. Quantities are given in individual directions. 5 double-pointed needles size 2 (Am) or 11 (Eng). Shoe-sock soles (buy a size larger than usual as the knitting will take up a size).

Basic Stitch: Rnds of st st (K every rnd).

To Turn Heel and Shape Toe: After the completion of leg as given in individual directions, continue thus: Leave sts on 2nd and 3rd needles and work across 1st and 4th needles in R of st st for given number of R.

Shape for Heel: Divide sts into 3 (placing colored threads between the sections), K across 1st section and across 2nd section to last st, K this st together with 1st st of third section through back of sts, K next st, turn, slip st and P across center section to last st, P this together with first st of next section, P 1, turn, slip 1 and work in this way until all side sts have been worked over. Pick up sts along sides of heel and divide all heel sts to 1st and 4th needles. Work a rnd over all sts, knitting through back of the side heel sts.

Shape for Instep: 1st needle: K to last 3 sts, K 2 together, K 1, K across 2nd and 3rd needles, then on 4th needle; K 1, K 2 together through back of sts, K to end. Continue thus, decreasing in every rnd as instructed. Work straight on remaining sts until toe is reached.

Shape Toe: 1st and 3rd needles: K to last 3 sts, K 2 together, K 1. 2nd and 4th needles: K 1, K 2 together through back of sts, K to end. Repeat as instructed until 8 sts remain. Graft or cast off these sts.

Tension: 30 sts and 40 R over pattern = 10 cm or 4".

Abbreviations: K = knit. P = purl. St(s) = stitch(es). R = row(s). Rnd(s) = round(s). St st = stocking or stockinette stitch.

Man's Socks

Size: 9–10 (Am) or $7\frac{1}{2}$–$8\frac{1}{2}$ (Eng).

Yarn Required: 100 gm or 4 oz green, 50 gm or 2 oz each red, yellow, white.

Knitting Chart 1: 8 sts and 26 rnds = 1 repeat.

DIRECTIONS

Using green, cast 18 sts onto each of 4 needles and work in K 1, P 1 rib on the 72 sts to 6 cm or $2\frac{1}{4}$". Now work the 1st–26th rnds of Knitting Chart 1. Work the heel in green on 36 sts for 24 R as described, then turn heel with 12 sts for each section until 24 sts remain. Using green, pick up 12 sts each side of heel and working on 84 sts, decrease for instep as given until 72 sts remain. Continue from Knitting Chart 1, beginning with the 4th Rnd. Work straight to 22 cm or $8\frac{1}{2}$" (or length required) measured from beginning of heel. Shape Toe by decreasing as stated in every 2nd rnd 8 times, then in every rnd 8 times.

Woman's Socks

Size: 8–9 (Am) or $4\frac{1}{2}$–6 (Eng).

Yarn Required: 100 gm or 4 oz blue, 50 gm or 2 oz each red, white, pale blue.

Color Sequence: *4 rnds blue, 2 rnds each white, pale blue, red, white, 4 rnds blue, 10 rnds Knitting Chart 2. Repeat from *.

DIRECTIONS

Using blue, cast 16 sts onto each of 4 needles and work in K 1, P 1 rib on the 64 sts to 12 cm or $4\frac{3}{4}$". Now repeat the Color Sequence 1 time. Work the heel in blue on 32 sts for 20 R, then turn heel with 12 sts in center section and 10 sts in side sections. Using blue, pick up 10 sts each side of heel and working on 74 sts, decrease for instep as given until 64 sts remain. Now work straight in Color Sequence 2 times. Continue in blue. Shape Toe, decreasing in every 2nd rnd 6 times, then in every rnd 8 times.

Child's Knee Socks

Size: 3–4 (Am) or $1\frac{1}{2}$–$2\frac{1}{2}$ (Eng).

Yarn Required: 100 gm or 4 oz yellow, 50 gm or 2 oz each red, blue, pale blue.

Color Sequence: *6 rnds yellow, 10 rnds Knitting Chart 3, repeat from *.

DIRECTIONS

Using yellow, cast 18 sts onto each of 4 needles and work in K 1, P 1 rib on the 72 sts for 4 cm or $1\frac{1}{2}$". Change to Basic Stitch and Color Sequence and work to 12 cm or $4\frac{1}{2}$". Keeping continuity of Color Sequence, shape for leg thus: On 1st needle, K 2 sts together, work to end of rnd. Work 1 rnd straight. In next rnd, work to last 2 sts of 4th needle, K 2 together through back of sts. Work 1 rnd straight. Repeat these 4 rnds 5 times more – 60 sts. Redistribute the sts by slipping 3 sts from beginning of 2nd needle to end of 1st needle, and 3 sts at end of 3rd needle to beginning of 4th needle – 15 sts on each needle. Work straight until Color Sequence has been worked

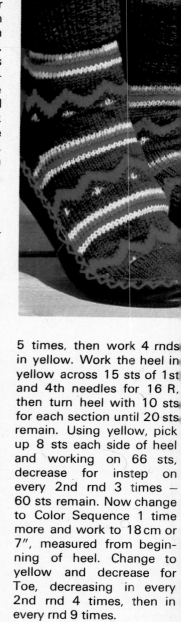

5 times, then work 4 rnds in yellow. Work the heel in yellow across 15 sts of 1st and 4th needles for 16 R, then turn heel with 10 sts for each section until 20 sts remain. Using yellow, pick up 8 sts each side of heel and working on 66 sts, decrease for instep on every 2nd rnd 3 times – 60 sts remain. Now change to Color Sequence 1 time more and work to 18 cm or 7", measured from beginning of heel. Change to yellow and decrease for Toe, decreasing in every 2nd rnd 4 times, then in every rnd 9 times.

Child's Shoe-Socks

Size: $12\frac{1}{2}$–$1\frac{1}{2}$ (Am) or 11–$12\frac{1}{2}$ (Eng).

Yarn Required: 50 gm or 2 oz each in red, green, yellow, and white.

These house socks will make perfect slip-ons to wear while relaxing in the evenings. Plastic foam insoles, together with the leather outer soles, give protection from cold floor surfaces.

Color Sequence: *4 rnds red, 11 rnds Knitting Chart 4, repeat from *.

DIRECTIONS

Using red, cast 12 sts onto each of 4 needles and work in K 1, P 1 rib on the 48 sts for 3 cm or 1¼".

Now repeat the Color Sequence 1 time, then work 2 rnds in red. Work the heel in red on 24 sts for 14 R, then turn heel with 8 sts in each section. Using red, pick up 7 sts each side of heel and working on 54 sts, decrease for gusset on every 2nd rnd 3 times — 48 sts. Now beginning with Knitting Chart 4, work Color Sequence until foot measures 15 cm or 6", measured from beginning of heel. Shape Toe by decreasing as stated in every 2nd rnd 2 times, then in every rnd 8 times.

Knitting Chart 1

26. Rnd
25. Rnd
24. Rnd
23. Rnd
22. Rnd
21. Rnd
20. Rnd
19. Rnd
18. Rnd
17. Rnd
16. Rnd
15. Rnd
14. Rnd
13. Rnd
12. Rnd
11. Rnd
10. Rnd
9. Rnd
8. Rnd
7. Rnd
6. Rnd
5. Rnd
4. Rnd
3. Rnd
2. Rnd
1. Rnd

1 Repeat

Knitting Chart 2

10. Rnd
9. Rnd
8. Rnd
7. Rnd
6. Rnd
5. Rnd
4. Rnd
3. Rnd
2. Rnd
1. Rnd

1 Repeat

Knitting Chart 3

10. Rnd
9. Rnd
8. Rnd
7. Rnd
6. Rnd
5. Rnd
4. Rnd
3. Rnd
2. Rnd
1. Rnd

1 Repeat

Knitting Chart 4

11. Rnd
10. Rnd
9. Rnd
8. Rnd
7. Rnd
6. Rnd
5. Rnd
4. Rnd
3. Rnd
2. Rnd
1. Rnd

1 Repeat

X	X	X	X	X	X
Yellow	Red	Pale blue	Blue	Green	White

Knitting Charts: One repeat is given for each design. Each cross represents one stitch in the color indicated in the color key given above. Chart 1 is for Man's Socks, Chart 2 is for Woman's Socks, Chart 3 is for Child's Knee Socks, and Chart 4 is for the Child's Shoe-Socks.

In bouclé and plain yarns
Patterned perfection

This eye-catching cardigan will win you many admiring glances. Quickly work the front and back in white bouclé, then take your time and enjoy knitting the sleeves in bright straight and zigzag stripes.

Size: Directions are for 88 cm or 34½" bust. Changes for 96 cm or 37½" bust are in brackets.

Materials Required:

Bouclé: 250 (300) gm or 9 (11) oz white [50 gm = 50 m or 54 yds].

Plain: 150 gm or 6 oz each of white and red, 50 gm or 2 oz each of blue and turquoise [50 gm = 100 m or 108 yds]. Knitting needles sizes 5 and 8 (Am) or 6 and 8 (Eng). 6 buttons.

Basic Pattern 1: With bouclé yarn and thicker needles, work in reverse st st.

Basic Pattern 2: With plain yarn and finer needles, work in st st from chart.

Tension 1: 13 sts and 23 R = 10 cm or 4" over bouclé.

Tension 2: 19 sts and 25 R = 10 cm or 4" over plain yarn.

Abbreviations: K = knit. P = purl. St(s) = stitch(es). R = row(s). St st = stocking or stockinette stitch.

DIRECTIONS

Back: Using plain red and finer needles, cast on 72 (80) sts and work 2 R red, 20 R white, and 3 R red in K 1, P 1 rib. Change to thicker needles and bouclé and K next R, decreasing 14 (18) sts evenly across R – 58 (62) sts. Continue in reverse st st to 33 cm or 13".

Shape Armholes: At beginning of every R, cast off 3 sts 2 times, 2 sts 2 times, 1 st 6 times – 42 (46) sts. Work straight to 50 (51) cm or 19½" (20").

Shape Neck and Shoulders: Cast off center 12 sts and work on each side separately. At neck edge, at beginning of every 2nd R cast off 2 sts 2 times and 1 st 1 time. *At the same time,* at 51 (52) cm or 20" (20½") at armhole edge, cast off 5 (6) sts in every 2nd R 2 times.

Left Front: Using plain red and finer needles, cast on 31 (35) sts and work rib as for Back. Change to thicker needles and bouclé and K next R (wrong side), decreasing 5 (7) sts evenly across R – 26

(28) sts. Continue in reverse st st, shaping armhole as for Back, then continue straight to 43 (44) cm or 17" (17½").

Shape Neck: At beginning of wrong side R, cast off 2 sts 2 times, then 1 st 2 times. Now decrease 1 st at front edge on every 4th R 2 times. *At the same time,* at 51 (52) cm or 20" (20½") shape shoulder as for Back.

Right Front: Work to match Left Front, reversing all shapings.

Sleeves: Using plain red and finer needles, cast on 37 (43) sts and work 8 cm or 3" in K 1, P 1 rib. Change to thicker needles and work in Basic Pattern 2 (Note: the white sts are shown in black). Repeat the 6 sts of pattern across R to last st, K edge st. Continue, repeating the 36 R and increasing 1 st each end of 6th and 8th R alternately 11 (12) times – 59 (67) sts. Work straight to 45 cm or 17¾".

Shape Top: At beginning of every R, cast off 3 sts 2 times, 2 sts 6 times, 1 st 16 times, 2 sts 6 (8) times, and 3 sts 2 times. Cast off.

Finishing: Join seams. Using finer needles and plain red, pick up 101 sts around neck and work in K 1, P 1 rib in 2 R red, 7 R white, and 2 R red. Cast off in red. Using red, pick up 95 (99) sts along Right Front edge and work in rib in color sequence as for neckband, making buttonholes in the 4th white R over 2 sts, placing the 1st one 2 cm or ¾" from lower edge, the 2nd one the same distance from neck edge, and 4 more at equal intervals between.

Work buttonband to match, omitting buttonholes. Sew on buttons.

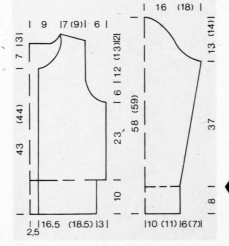

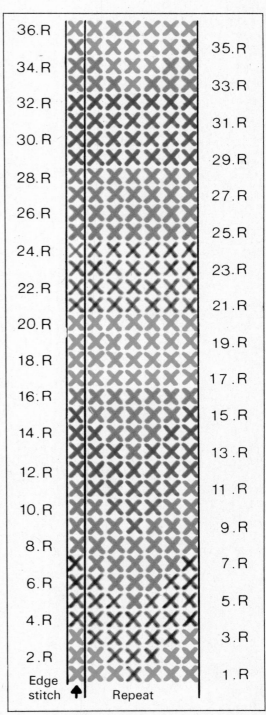

◄ **Half-pattern for small (large) size. The numbers are centimeters; inches are in directions.**

▲ **Knitting Chart: Each x = 1 st in that color. Read odd-numbered rows from right to left and even-numbered rows from left to right.**

Graphic design

Size: Directions are for 88 cm or 34½" bust. Changes for 96 cm or 37½" bust are in brackets.

Materials Required:

Coat: 950 (1000) gm or 34 (36) oz white, 250 gm or 9 oz rust, 150 gm or 6 oz purple, 100 gm or 4 oz each of blue and black. Hat: 50 gm or 2 oz white, small amounts of rust, purple, blue, and black [50 gm = 70 m or 80 yds]. Both: Knitting needles size 7 (Am and Eng). Circular needles sizes 7 and 8 (Am) or 6 and 7 (Eng). St holders. 7 buttons. Fabric for pocket linings.

Basic Stitch: St st.

Knitting Chart: 1 repeat of pattern, plus end st are given. Black cross = white, Colored crosses = 1 st in relevant color. Only the right side R are shown.

Color Sequence of secondary colors: * rust, blue, rust, purple, repeat from *.

Stripe Sequence: With circular needle, work back and forth in open rows of st st, beginning the R where the relevant color is hanging. *3 R white; 2 R each rust and white; 2 R black, working pattern for the 1st of these 2 rows by working 3 sts, then slip next st purlwise. In next R, slip the slipped st and work the 3 sts. Then work 2 R white, 2 R purple or blue, 4 R white, 2 R garter st in the secondary color of the following Knitting Chart pattern (see photograph), 20 R from Knitting Chart, 2 R garter st in white, 3 R st st in white, 2 R each rust and white. Work 2 R black as before, but stagger the slipped st by moving 2 sts to the right of previous slip-st R. Work 2 R white and 2 R blue or purple. Repeat from *, working the last stripe of the Stripe Sequence in purple before the blue Knitting Chart pattern and in blue before the purple Knitting Chart pattern.

Tension: 18 sts and 25 R = 10 cm or 4".

Abbreviations: K = knit. P = purl. St(s) = stitch(es). St st = stocking or stockinette st. R = row(s).

COAT

Back: Using knitting needles and white, cast on 116 (124) sts and work 6 cm or 2½" in garter st. Change to the thicker circular needle and work in Stripe Sequence, but begin the first repeat with only 2 R white instead of 3. Decrease 1 st each end of 6th R, then each end of every 12th R 12 times. Note: Work Knitting Chart pattern over 112 (120) sts thus: 5th R of chart will read: K 1 (edge st), repeat sts 1 (9)–12 1 time, sts 1–12 8 (9) times, sts 1–4 for larger size only, for both sizes sts 13–14, K 1 (edge st). Keeping continuity of pattern, work to 47 cm or 18½". To work pocket opening, at beginning of next 2 R, cast on 4 sts, then still decreasing at side edge as before, continue for 16 cm or 6¼". At beginning of next 2 R, cast off 4 sts. When decreases are completed and 90 (98) sts remain, continue straight to 89 cm or 35".

Shape Armholes: At beginning of next 2 R, cast off 8 sts and continue straight on the 74 (82) sts to 108 (109) cm or 42½" (43").

Shape Neck: Cast off cent[er] 22 sts and work on ea[ch] side separately. At ne[ck] edge, in every 2nd R ca[st] off 2 sts 2 times, then ca[st] off remaining 22 (26) sts [on] next armhole edge R.

Right Front: Using knittin[g] needles and white, cast o[n] 55 (59) sts and work [in] garter st for 6 cm or 2½[".] Change to the thick[er] circular needle and work [in] Stripe Sequence, workin[g] side decreases, pock[et] edge, armhole, and shoulde[r] as for Back. Work fro[m] edge straight, and work th[e] 5th R of Knitting Cha[rt] pattern over 53 (57) s[ts] thus: K 1 (edge st), repea[t] sts 1–12 4 times, then s[ts] 1–3 (7) 1 time, K 1 (edg[e] st). Shape front slope at 9[2] (96) cm or 37¼" (37¾") [by] decreasing 1 st at beginnin[g] of next front edge R and a[t] same edge on every 3rd [R] 11 times.

Left Front: Work as fo[r] Right Front, reversing a[ll] shapings and placing of st[s] for Knitting Chart pattern.

Sleeves: Using knittin[g] needles and white, cast o[n] 74 (76) sts and work i[n] garter st for 8 cm or 3[".] Change to the thicke[r] circular needle and work i[n] Stripe Sequence, beginnin[g] with 4 R white, then 2 [R] garter st in rust. For Knittin[g] Chart, R 5 will read: wor[k] sts 1–12 6 times, then st[s] 13–14 1 time (for large[r] size work K 1 each end[)]. Continue in pattern to 48 cm or 19". Cast off.

Right Band with Collar: Using the finer circula[r] needle, cast on 200 (202[)] sts and work back and fort[h] in garter st to 2.5 cm or 1[".] Work buttonholes in next [R] over 3 sts, placing 1st one [at] 16 cm or 6" from right edg[e] and 5 more at 8 cm or 3[½"] intervals. In next R, cast o[n] 3 sts in place of those cas[t] off. Work to 5 cm or 2[",] ending at left edge. Cast o[ff] 170 (172) sts at beginnin[g] of next R, then at same edge, decrease 1 st ever[y] 10th R 7 times. Work o[n]

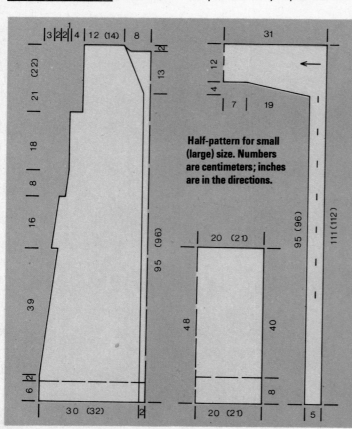

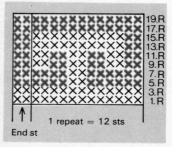

Knitting Chart: 1 repeat of the pattern, plus end sts are given. Black x = 1 st white, colored x = 1 st in that color. Right side R are given; P all wrong side R in colors of previous R.

Half-pattern for small (large) size. Numbers are centimeters; inches are in the directions.

remaining 23 sts to 31 cm or 12¼″, measured from cast-on edge. Place sts on st holder.

Left Band with Collar: Work as for other Band, omitting buttonholes (work is reversible).

Finishing: Press carefully. Pin center of Sleeve top to shoulder seam, then sew in Sleeves. Join all seams. Make pocket linings from fabric and sew in place. Graft the two sets of sts on Collar, then sew on Collar and Bands neatly. Sew on buttons.

HAT

Using knitting needles and white, cast on 92 sts and work 8 R in garter st. Change to the thicker circular needle and Stripe Sequence, but omit the Knitting Chart pattern and garter st R. Change to white and decrease thus: K 1, *K 1, K 2 together through back of loop, K 9, K 2 together, K 1. Repeat from * 5 times more, K 1 — 80 sts.

Continue to decrease thus on every 2nd R 4 times more, working 2 sts less between decreases — 32 sts remain. In next alternate R, K 1, *K 1, slip 2, K 1, pass slip sts over, K 1, repeat from * 5 times, K 1 — 20 sts. Work 1 R, break yarn, and thread through the remaining sts. Draw up tightly and sew seam.

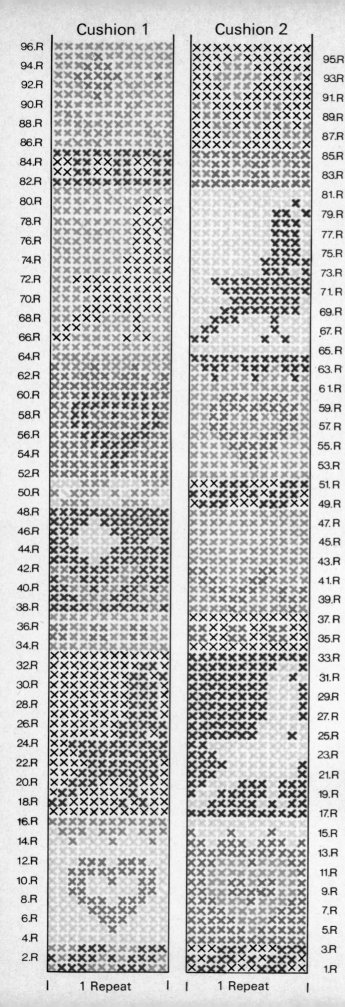

Cushion 1 — 1 Repeat

Cushion 2 — 1 Repeat

Row numbers for Cushion 1 (left): 2.R, 4.R, 6.R, 8.R, 10.R, 12.R, 14.R, 16.R, 18.R, 20.R, 22.R, 24.R, 26.R, 28.R, 30.R, 32.R, 34.R, 36.R, 38.R, 40.R, 42.R, 44.R, 46.R, 48.R, 50.R, 52.R, 54.R, 56.R, 58.R, 60.R, 62.R, 64.R, 66.R, 68.R, 70.R, 72.R, 74.R, 76.R, 78.R, 80.R, 82.R, 84.R, 86.R, 88.R, 90.R, 92.R, 94.R, 96.R

Row numbers for Cushion 2 (right): 1.R, 3.R, 5.R, 7.R, 9.R, 11.R, 13.R, 15.R, 17.R, 19.R, 21.R, 23.R, 25.R, 27.R, 29.R, 31.R, 33.R, 35.R, 37.R, 39.R, 41.R, 43.R, 45.R, 47.R, 49.R, 51.R, 53.R, 55.R, 57.R, 59.R, 61.R, 63.R, 65.R, 67.R, 69.R, 71.R, 73.R, 75.R, 77.R, 79.R, 81.R, 83.R, 85.R, 87.R, 89.R, 91.R, 93.R, 95.R

Cushion 1

Cushion 2

Cushi

Motif medle

Bands of bright motifs add up to the most colorful cushions around. Worked in stocking or stockinette stitch, they are a marvelous way to use up remnants of yarn.

Size: 40 cm or 16" square.
Materials Required:

Cushions 1 and 2: 100 gm or 4 oz dark blue, 20 gm or 1 oz each red, pale blue, yellow, green, and white.
Cushions 3 and 4: 100 gm or 4 oz red, 20 gm or 1 oz each dark blue, pale blue, yellow, green, and white [100 gm = 400 m or 437 yds]. Knitting needles sizes 2 (Am) or 11 (Eng).

Basic Stitch: St st.
Tension: 30 sts and 36 R = 10 cm or 4".
Abbreviations: R = row(s). St(s) = stitch(es). K = kni St st = stocking or stock inette stitch.

DIRECTIONS

Front: Using the color of th 1st R, cast on 120 sts fo each cushion cover and K 1 in the same color. Now wor in Basic Stitch, following th Knitting Charts and workin R 1–96 1 time, then R 1–4 1 time – 145 R in all. K 1 R color of last R, then cast of

Back: Work same number o R as for Front, but wor Cushions 1 and 2 in dar blue and Cushions 3 and in red.

Finishing: Press work wit warm iron over damp cloth Join seams on 3 sides, inse cushion, then sew up remain ing seam.

Cushion 4

Cushion 3

Cushion 4

Practise your patterning with a set of cushions. There are two designs, each repeated in two color variations. The traditional motifs suit simple cottage furniture.

Knitting Chart: 1 repeat of the pattern is given; every colored cross equals one stitch in that color. The color key is given below:

✕	= Pale blue
✕	= Green
✕	= Red
✕	= Yellow
✕	= Dark blue
✕	= White

Cushion 3 row labels (left side): 96.R 94.R 92.R 90.R 88.R 86.R 84.R 82.R 80.R 78.R 76.R 74.R 72.R 70.R 68.R 66.R 64.R 62.R 60.R 58.R 56.R 54.R 52.R 50.R 48.R 46.R 44.R 42.R 40.R 38.R 36.R 34.R 32.R 30.R 28.R 26.R 24.R 22.R 20.R 18.R 16.R 14.R 12.R 10.R 8.R 6.R 4.R 2.R

Cushion 4 row labels (right side): 95.R 93.R 91.R 89.R 87.R 85.R 83.R 81.R 79.R 77.R 75.R 73.R 71.R 69.R 67.R 65.R 63.R 61.R 59.R 57.R 55.R 53.R 51.R 49.R 47.R 45.R 43.R 41.R 39.R 37.R 35.R 33.R 31.R 29.R 27.R 25.R 23.R 21.R 19.R 17.R 15.R 13.R 11.R 9.R 7.R 5.R 3.R 1.R

1 Repeat 1 Repeat

2079

Size: 80 cm or 31½" square.
Materials Required:

Colors and quantities are in individual directions [100 gm = 62 m or 68 yds]. Knitting needles size 10½ (Am) or 2 (Eng).
Basic Stitch: St st.
Tension: 12 sts and 13 R = 10 cm or 4".
Abbreviations: K = knit. P = purl. St(s) = stitch(es). St st = stocking or stockinette st. R = row(s).

CUSHION 1

Yarn: 1300 gm or 46 oz brown, 400 gm or 15 oz ecru.
DIRECTIONS
Using brown, cast on 95 sts and P 1 R. Work in st st and follow Chart 1 thus: K 1 (edge st), repeat sts 1–10 9 times, sts 1–3 1 time, K 1 (edge st). Continue to work as set, repeating R 1–22 4 times, then R 1–15 1 time. P next R in brown, then work 104 R in st st in brown. Cast off.

CUSHION 2

Yarn: 1200 gm or 43 oz brown, 400 gm or 15 oz ecru.
DIRECTIONS
Using brown, cast on 95 sts and work 3 R in st st, beginning with a P R. Continue in st st, following Chart 2 thus: K 1 (edge st), repeat sts 1–14 6 times, sts 1–9 1 time, K 1 (edge st). Continue to work as set repeating R 1–14 7 times, then R 1 1 time. Work 108 R in brown. Cast off.

CUSHION 3

Yarn: 1200 gm or 43 oz ecru, 400 gm or 15 oz brown.
DIRECTIONS
Using ecru, cast on 95 sts and P 1 R. Work in st st following Chart 3 thus: K 1 (edge st), repeat sts 1–20 4 times, sts 1–13 1 time, K 1 (edge st). Continue to work as set, repeating R 1–15 6 times, then R 1–11 1 time. Work 104 R in ecru. Cast off.

Finishing: Pin out and press on wrong side. Fold in half, right sides facing, join side seams, turn to right side, and press seams. Insert cushion; sew seam.

Chart 1

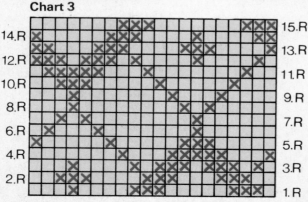

Chart 2

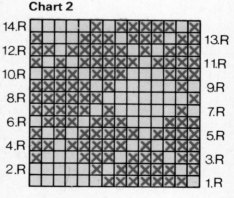

Chart 3

Knitting Charts:
1 repeat of the pattern (as seen from the right side) is given. Read the chart from right to left on right side rows and from left to right on the wrong side rows.

At floor level

Create a cozy corner for relaxing in your living room with a trio of unusual cushions. Each has a different two-tone pattern in shades of brown, which will blend with most decors.

2

3

1

Blackberry stitch

1 From the wrong side, work into the back, the front, the back, and the front of next stitch to make four stitches.

2 Turn the piece and knit these same four stitches, then turn the piece again and purl the same four stitches.

3 Now slip the second stitch over the first, then the third stitch and finally the fourth stitch are slipped over – one stitch remains.

4 Place the Blackberry Stitch on the right-hand needle and then pattern across row, following the Knitting Diagram.

Cable comfort

Display traditional Aran designs to maximum advantage with this stunning knitted bedspread. Use it to complement furniture of natural materials like wood.

Size: About 240cm x 150 cm or 94" x 60" (made in 3 strips).

Materials Required:

1050gm or 38oz per strip [50gm = 140m or 153 yds]. Knitting needles size 10 (Am) or 4 (Eng). Cable needle.

Basic Pattern: See Knitting Diagram. The right half of the pattern for each strip (minus edge st) is shown, plus center st. The other half is worked in reverse. Diagram shows the 1st R, (wrong side and increase R), and from then only the right side R are given. In all wrong side R, work the sts as they appear, working the twisted sts purlwise. When working the large cables, reverse the cables on the second side of strip by placing sts on cable needle and leaving them at back of work. For the center motif and the large cable, repeat from 4th –31st R, but for the small cable and rope cable, repeat from the 4th–27th R inclusive.

Explanation of signs: 2 + 2 sts crossed to the left = slip 2 sts onto cable needle and leave at front of work, K next 2 sts, then K 2 sts from cable needle. 2 + 2 sts crossed to the right = slip 2 sts onto cable needle and leave at back of work, K next 2 sts, then K 2 sts from cable needle. 1 + 2 sts crossed to the right = slip 1 st o[n] cable needle and leave a[t] back, K next 2 sts then [K] the cable needle st. 2 + [1] st crossed to left = sli[p] 2 sts on cable needle an[d] leave at front of work, [K] next st, then K the cabl[e] needle sts. Increase 1 s[t] in Twisted Purl = P int[o] back and then front of s[t.] Twisted Knit Stitch = [K] into back of st. For Black[-] berry Stitch see How-to.

Border Pattern: See Knitting Diagram. Half a stri[p] plus center st is shown[.] The other half is worked i[n] reverse. Spaces are show[n] as guide for increases i[n] 1st R of Basic Pattern[.] The 2 R of Border Patter[n] are repeated.

Tension: 19 sts and 21 [R] = 10cm or 4".

Abbreviations: K = knit[.] P = purl. St(s) = stitch(es[).] R = row(s).

DIRECTIONS

3 strips required. For eac[h] strip, cast on 93 sts. K 1 s[t] each end as edge st, the[n] follow the Border Patter[n] and work 6 R. Continue i[n] Basic Pattern, increasin[g] 10 sts evenly across 1st R [–] 103 sts. Continue i[n] pattern, keeping 1 st eac[h] end in K for edge st (no[t] shown) and work unti[l] strip measures 240cm o[r] 94", working the last 6 R i[n] Border Pattern and decreas[-] ing the last Basic Pattern [R] by 10 sts to correspon[d] with the beginning. Cast of[f.] **Finishing:** Join the strip[s] together neatly from wron[g] side. Press seams.

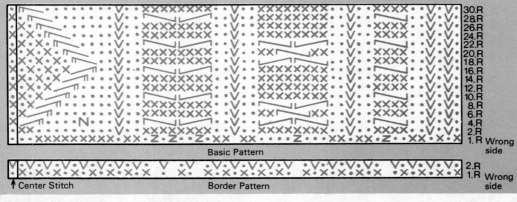

Knitting Diagram: The right half of the pattern for each strip, plus the center stitch is given. The other half is worked in reverse.

x = K 1 st

• = P 1 st

Z = Increase 1 st in Twisted Purl

V = 1 Twisted Knit Stitch

N = 1 Blackberry Stitch

= 2 + 2 crossed to left

= 2 + 2 crossed to right

= 1 + 2 crossed to right

= 2 + 1 crossed to left

30.R
28.R
26.R
24.R
22.R
20.R
18.R
16.R
14.R
12.R
10.R
8.R
6.R
4.R
2.R
1.R Wrong side

Basic Pattern

2.R
1.R Wrong side

↑ Center Stitch   Border Pattern

If you are young and slim, wear this deliciously brief bikini with its own matching jacket.

Crochet

Get set for the summer

Size: Directions are for 84 cm or 33" bust. Changes for 92 cm or 36" bust are in brackets.

Materials Required:

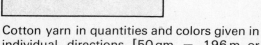

Cotton yarn in quantities and colors given in individual directions [50 gm = 196 m or 214 yds]. Crochet hook size C.

Abbreviations: Ch = chain. St(s) = stitch(es). Sc = single crochet. Hdc = half double crochet. Dc = double crochet. R = row(s). Rnd(s) = round(s).

STYLE 1

Materials Required: Jacket: 300 (350) gm or 11 (13) oz blue, 50 gm or 2 oz white. Bikini: 100 (150) gm or 4 (6) oz blue, small amount white. 25 large glass beads. Narrow elastic for beads.

Basic Pattern: Jacket: Hdc, turning each R with 2 ch. Bikini: Sc, turning each R with 1 ch.

Tension: Jacket: 27 sts and 19 R = 10 cm or 4". Bikini: 27 sts and 34 R = 10 cm or 4".

Crochet Motif: See How-to, Style 1, photographs 1–4.

DIRECTIONS

Jacket: Back and Front: Work in one to armholes. Make 267 (291) ch and work 1 hdc into 2nd ch from hook, then 2 hdc into next 2 ch, *1 motif, 3 hdc, repeat from * to end — 11 (12) motifs. Continue to work Crochet Motifs with 3 hdc at each end.

When Crochet Motifs are completed, continue in hdc across all sts — 213 (231) hdc. Now mark the 51st (56th) hdc from each edge as "side seam". At these marked points, decrease 1 st in every 2nd R 10 times — 193 (211) sts. Work straight to 23 cm or 9" then at "side seams" increase 1 st in every 4th R 10 times — 213 (231) sts. Continue straight to 45 cm or 17¾". Leave Right and Left Front sts and work on Back 111 (119) hdc.

Shape Armholes: Decrease 4 sts each end of next R by slip-stitching along to 5th hdc, then work in

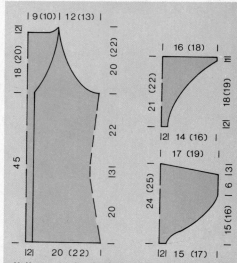

Half-patterns for the Style 1 bikini and jacket in the small (large) size. The numbers are centimeters; inch equivalents are given in the directions.

2084

The yarn is cotton in blue and white. Beads are threaded onto elastic to secure the halter neck straps and the sides of the bikini pants.

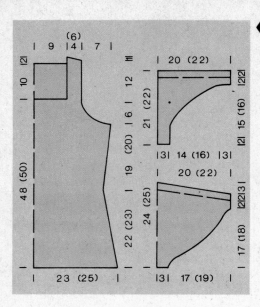

◀ Half-patterns for Style 2 bikini and slipover. The numbers are centimeters; inches are in the directions.

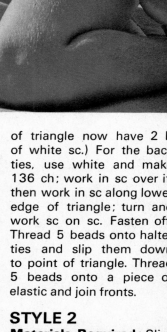

This little slipover top will be very useful. The pattern is cool-looking and the color will show off your tan.

hdc to last 4 hdc, turn. Decrease 4 sts each end of next R, 2 sts each end of next 5 R, 1 st each end of next 6 (9) R, then 1 st each end of every 2nd R 4 times, 1 st each end of every 3rd R 3 (2) times. *At the same time,* at 63 (65) cm or 24¾" (25½"), leave center 39 (43) sts unworked and work on each side separately. At neck edge, decrease 2 sts every 2nd R 2 times and 1 st 1 time.

Left Front: Shape armhole to correspond with Back. *At the same time,* shape front edge by decreasing 1 st on next 2 R, then 1 st on every 2nd R 18 (21) times. Fasten off.

Right Front: Work to match Left Front, reversing shapings.

Finishing: Join shoulders with just one stitch. Work in sc around armholes, working 1 rnd blue and 2 rnds white. Fasten off. Work 1 R blue sc all around outer edges, then work 2 R white along straight edges of front and lower edge. Fasten off. Using white, make 110 ch and work 1 R of sc, now join to neck edge and work 1 row of sc around neck edge, work another 110 ch, work 1 R of sc into this ch, and work sc on sc around neck edge. Fasten off.

Pants: Back: Make 11 ch and work sc into 2nd ch from hook, then sc in each ch to end. Now work in sc, increasing 1 st each end of every 2nd R 4 times, then 1 st each end of next 2 R, 2 sts each end of next 3 R, then increase 1 st and 2 sts each end alternately 7 (10) times, 1 st each end of next 6 R, and 1 st each end of every 2nd R 13 times — 92 (102) sc. Work straight to 21 (22 cm) or 8¼" (8½").

Shape Back: Continue in sc, but work across 9 (10) sts less each end of next 9 R. Fasten off.

Front: Make 11 ch and work foundation R as for Back, then work in sc to 2 cm or ¾". Increase 1 st each end of every 3rd R 5 times, 1 st each end of every 2nd R 13 (11) times, and 1 st each end of next 20 (27) R — 86 (96) sc. Work 1 cm or ½". Fasten off.

Finishing: Join crotch seam. Work 1 R sc in blue and 2 R in white along each leg, easing in the back curve slightly.

On upper edges of Back and Front work 2 R of sc in white. Fasten off. Take 2 pieces of elastic 5 cm or 2" long and thread 5 beads onto each piece. Join sides with this elastic.

Top: Left half: Make 46 (50) ch in blue and work 16 (18) hdc, 7 ch, skip 10 ch, 10 dc in next st, miss 10 ch, 7 ch, 7 (9) hdc (front edge). Continue to work motif as for Jacket, increasing as before on hdc, by working 1 hdc extra each side of motif. *At the same time,* at left edge decrease 1 hdc on every 2nd R and at right edge decrease 1 hdc every R until 3 hdc remain. Work 3 hdc together.

Right half: Work as for Left Half, but reversing shapings.

Finishing: First work 1 R of sc in blue along side edges of triangles. Fasten off. Work 2 R of sc in white along inner edge of triangle. Fasten off. For halter ties, use white and make 136 ch; turn and work 1 row sc, then work in sc along outer edge of triangle to lower edge; turn and work in sc. (Both sides of triangle now have 2 R of white sc.) For the back ties, use white and make 136 ch; work in sc over it, then work in sc along lower edge of triangle; turn and work sc on sc. Fasten off. Thread 5 beads onto halter ties and slip them down to point of triangle. Thread 5 beads onto a piece of elastic and join fronts.

STYLE 2

Materials Required: Slipover: 200 (250) gm or 8 (9) oz turquoise. Bikini: 100 (150) gm or 4 (6) oz turquoise.

Basic Pattern: Slipover. R 1: 1 dc into 6th ch from hook, *4 ch, skip 3 sts, 1 sc in next st, 4 ch, skip 3 sts, then 1 dc, 2 ch, 1 dc in next st, repeat from *. R 2: See How-to, Style 2, photograph 1. R 3: See How-to,

This second bikini co-ordinates with the slipover on the opposite page. The darts in the bra ensure a good fit.

Style 2, photograph 2. Repeat R 2 and 3. **Bikini:** Sc, turning each R with 1 ch.

Tension: <u>Slipover</u>: 3½–3¾ groups and 13 R = 10 cm or 4". <u>Bikini</u>: 27 sts and 34 R = 10 cm or 4".

DIRECTIONS

Slipover: <u>Back</u>: Using turquoise, make 126 (134) ch and work in Basic Pattern – 15½ (16½) groups. Repeat 2nd and 3rd R 1 time more, but do not turn with ch. Decrease ½ group each end by slip-stitching along "V", then 7 ch, work in pattern to last "V", sc into "V", turn with 2 ch, then 4 ch, 1 sc into center of loop, and work in pattern, ending 4 ch, 1 sc in center loop, 4 ch, 1 sc in end st. Continue in pattern for 4 R, thus ending after 3rd

pattern R, then slip-stitch along to "V" and continue in pattern to "V", turn – 13½ (14½) groups. Repeat these 12 R 1 time more, work straight on the 11½ (12½) groups for 5 R, then increase ½ group each end of next and following 12th R – 13½ (14½) groups. Continue straight until work measures 41 (43) cm or 16¼" (17"), ending after a 3rd pattern R.

<u>Shape Armholes</u>: Decrease ½ pattern each end of next R, work 1 R straight, then decrease ½ group at each end of next R, work 1 R straight, repeat these 4 R until you have 9½ (10½) groups. Work straight until work measures 58 (60) cm or 22¾" (23½"). Pattern across 1½ groups, turn and work to end. Decrease ½ group at shoul-

der edge on next 2 R. Fasten off. Join yarn 1½ groups from end and work to match other shoulder.

<u>Front</u>: Work to match Back, but work on shoulder straps at 48 (50) cm or 19" (19½"), and work straight on 1½ groups until same length as Back to shoulder; shape shoulder as for Back.

<u>Finishing</u>: Pin out parts, cover with damp cloth, and leave to dry. Join side and shoulder seams. Work 1 rnd of sc around armholes, turn, and work 1 sc, * 1 picot in next st, 1 sc on next sc. Repeat from * all around. Fasten off.

Pants: <u>Back</u>: Make 15 ch and work in sc, then at each end increase 1 st every 2nd R 4 times, then in every R 1 st 2 times, 2 sts 3 times, then 1 st

and 2 sts alternately 7 (10) times, 1 st 6 times, in every 2nd R 1 st 15 times and 2 sts 2 times – 108 (118) sc. Work straight to 19 (20) cm or 7½" (8").

<u>Shape Back</u>: Continue in sc, but work 10 (11) sts less at each end of next 9 R. Work 1 R of sc across all sts, then work 1 R of crossed dc thus: Turn with 4 ch, *yarn over hook 2 times, insert hook into next st and draw through 2 loops, yarn over hook, skip 2 sts, insert hook into following st and draw yarn through 2 loops 4 times, 2 ch, yarn over hook, insert hook into top of dc and draw yarn through 2 loops 2 times. Repeat from *, ending with 1 tr into the last st. Work 3 R of sc, working 4 sc into each group. Fasten off.

Front: Make 15 ch and work in sc, increasing at each end 1 st every 4th R 4 times, 1 st every 2nd R 5 times, 1 st every R 11 (14) times, then every 2nd R 2 sts 2 (3) times, 5 sts 3 times, and 8 sts 1 time — 108 (118) sc. Work straight for 2 cm or ¾", then work 1 R of crossed dc and 3 R of sc. Fasten off.

Finishing: Join seams. Work 1 rnd of sc around each leg, easing in the back curve slightly.

Top: Right Half: Work in 2 pieces to form dart. For right piece, work 20 (23) ch and work in sc. Increase at left edge (dart edge) on every 3rd R 5 times. At the same time, at right outside edge, *decrease 1 st on every 2nd R 2 times, then 1 st on next R, repeat from * and work to 5 cm or 2", ending at dart edge. Put aside.

For left piece, make 28 (31) ch and on right edge (dart edge) increase 1 st every 3rd R. At the same time, at outside edge, * decrease 1 st in next 3 R, then 1 st in following 2nd R, repeat from * to 5 cm or 2", ending at dart edge, then join by working across right piece. Continue across all sts, decreasing as before until 3 sc remain. Decrease 3 together and fasten off.

Left Half: Work to match Right Half, reversing shapings.

Finishing: Join darts. Work 1 R of sc and 1 R of crossed dc along top edges. Make 135 ch for back strap; work 1 R of sc. Connect by a slip-stitch to lower edge of Right Half and work in sc along lower edge to end, work 6 ch, then work in sc along lower edge of Left Half, and at end make 135 ch, turn. Work in sc over all sts for 3 R. Fasten off.

For halter ties, make two lengths of 135 ch and work 3 R of sc. Fasten off. Sew into position at the top of the triangles.

How-to

Bikini patterns

Style 1

1 Each motif lies in between the number of half double crochets given in the directions. R 1: Work 7 ch, skip 10 sts, 10 dc into the next st, 7 ch, skip next 10 sts.

2 R 2: Work 4 ch, then work 15 dc into the next 10 dc by working (2 dc into the next dc, then 1 dc into the following dc) 5 times, and then end with 4 ch.

3 R 3: Work 4 ch, then work 23 dc into the next 15 dc by working (2 dc into the next dc, then 1 dc into the following dc) 7 times and finally 2 dc into last dc, 4 ch. R 4: 2 ch, 1 sc into first dc, *2 ch, skip 1 dc, 1 sc into next dc, repeat from the * to the end of the motif, then ch 2.

4 Work 1 more hdc before each motif, work (2 ch, 1 sc) into each 2-ch loop to the end of the motif, work 1 more hdc into the end group of hdc, 2 ch. In each row, there will be 1 less loop. When there are no loops left, motif is complete. Next row: 3 hdc into sc.

Style 2

1 R 1: Work as given in the Basic Pattern in the directions. R 2 (and all wrong side rows): *Work 1 sc into the ch space between dc, 1 picot (i.e. 4 ch, 1 sc into first ch to form loop), 1 sc, 1 picot, 1 sc into same space, 7 ch, repeat from *, ending with a picot group worked into the turning-ch space.

2 R 3: (and all right side rows): Begin with 5 ch and 1 dc into the sc between the picots, *work 4 ch, 1 sc into the center of the 7-ch loop, 4 ch, then (1 dc, 2 ch, 1 dc) into the sc between the picots, repeat from the * to the end of the row, turn with 2 ch. Repeat R 2 and 3 to required length.

Size: 42 cm or 16½" in diameter.

Materials Required:

280 gm or 10 oz white [50 gm = 155 m or 169 yds]. Crochet hook size D. Thick cotton cord for handle 140 cm or 55".

Abbreviations:
Ch = chain. Sc = single crochet. Hdc = half double crochet. Dc = double crochet. Tr = treble. St(s) = stitch(es). R = row(s). Rnd(s) = round(s).

DIRECTIONS

Back and Front (alike): Make 5 ch and join into a ring with a slip st.

Rnd 1: 1 ch (counted as 1st sc), 7 sc in ring, join with a slip st. Rnd 2: 3 ch (as 1st dc), 1 dc in same st, 1 ch, then (2 dc into next sc, 1 ch) 7 times, join with a slip st. (Join with a slip st at end of every rnd). Rnd 3: 3 ch, 2 dc in next dc, 2 ch, (1 dc in dc, 2 dc in next dc, 2 ch) 7 times — 24 dc. Rnd 4: 3 ch, 1 dc in 1st dc, 2 dc in next dc, 3 ch, (1 dc in each of next 2 dc, 2 dc in next dc, 3 ch) 7 times — 32 dc. Rnds 5–8: Repeat Rnd 4, always working 2 dc into last dc of every dc group and working 3 ch between groups of Rnds 5 and 6 and 4 ch between dc groups of Rnds 7 and 8. Rnd 9: 3 ch, 3 dc, 4 ch, 4 dc, 4 ch, (4 dc, 4 ch, 4 dc, 4 ch) 7 times. Rnd 10: 1 ch, 12 tr into next ch loop, 1 sc in last dc of dc group, 5 ch, (1 sc into 1st dc of next group, 12 tr into next loop, 1 sc on last dc, 5 ch) 7 times. Rnd 11: (1 sc into 1st tr, 2 ch and 1 sc into each tr — 11 loops now worked — then 2 ch, 3 hdc into the center 3 ch of 5-ch loop of Rnd 10, 2 ch) 8 times.

Do not join with a slip st from now on, but work round and round.

Rnd 12: (Work 1 sc, 2 ch into each of the 11 loops of previous rnd — 10 loops now worked — then 3 hdc into 3 hdc, 2 ch) 8 times. Rnd 13: (Work 1 sc, 2 ch into each of the 10 loops of previous rnd — 9 loops now worked — then 5 hdc into 3 hdc, 2 ch) 8 times. Rnd 14: (Work 1 sc, 2 ch into each of the 9 loops, 5 hdc into hdc, 2 ch) 8 times. Rnd 15–17: Repeat Rnd 14, but work 1 loop less in each rnd and work 6 hdc into each hdc group. Rnd 18: (4 loops as before, 8 hdc, 2 ch) 8 times. Rnd 19: (3 loops, 10 hdc, 2 ch) 8 times. Rnd 20: (2 loops, 14 hdc, 2 ch) 8 times. Rnd 21: (1 loop, 19 hdc, 2 ch) 8 times. Rnd 22: (1 dc in loop, 2 ch, 24 hdc, 2 ch) 8 times. Rnd 23: (1 dc in dc, 2 dc in ch loop, 27 hdc in hdc, 2 dc in ch loop) 7 times, 1 dc in dc, 2 dc in ch loop, 26 hdc in hdc, 2 dc in loop, join with slip st. Fasten off.

Mark 13 dc each side of 26 hdc and leave unworked. Join yarn to next dc from marked position and work on remaining dc in R thus: R 1: 3 ch, then dc in dc, working 2 dc into every 8th dc, turn with 3 ch. R 2: In dc, turn with 3 ch. R 3: In dc, working 2 dc into every 10th st. Fasten off.

Go back to the 52 sts left unworked. Join yarn and work 8 R of sc, joining each R to side edges of dc R. Fasten off.

Gusset: Make 16 ch and work 92 cm or 36" in sc. Fasten off.

Finishing: Join gusset between the 2 pieces with sc, beginning and ending 5 cm or 2" from the sc part. For straps, cut two 70 cm or 27½" lengths of cord and bind the ends. Chain a piece wide enough to fit around the cord and work in sc for 70 cm or 27½". Fasten off. Sew strip around cord. Sew straps to gusset at each side of opening.

In practical cotton
Summer round-up

Looking for the perfect summer bag? It's here, crocheted in bright cotton, with a flowery motif on the circular sides.

See through it

Lift a cotton blouse out of the ordinary with a delicate crocheted yoke and cuffs edged with scallops.

Size: Directions are for 84 cm or 33" bust. Changes for 92 cm or 36" bust are in brackets.

Materials Required:

50 gm or 2 oz crochet cotton. Crochet hook size 2. Fabric: 2.30 m or 2½ yds, 90 cm or 36" wide. 6 small buttons.

Basic Pattern: R 1: 1 sc in 6th st from hook, *5 ch, skip 2 ch, 1 sc in next st, repeat from * to end. R 2: 4 ch for turn, 1 sc in 1st space, *5 ch, 1 sc in next space, repeat from * to end. Repeat R 2.

Crochet Rosette: Make 5 ch and join into a ring with a slip st. Rnd 1: *10 ch, 1 sc in circle, repeat from * 7 times more. Cut yarn. Rnd 2: Begin again at point of 1st petal. Into 1st point, work 1 slip st, 5 ch. Continue all around, joining each point with a slip st with 5 ch between, ending 1 slip st in 1st slip st. Rnd 3: 1 ch, *in next space work (2 sc, 1 picot) 3 times, 2 sc. (Picot is 3 ch, then 1 sc into 1st of 3 ch). Repeat from * all around, ending with 1 slip st in 1st ch. Rnd 4: 3 ch (as 1st dc), *4 ch, 1 dc in center picot of group, 4 ch, 1 dc in last sc of group, 4 ch, 1 slip st in 3rd of beginning ch. Rnd 5: Work in slip st to next dc, 3 ch, then 9 dc in the same dc, *2 ch, skip 1 dc, 10 dc in next dc. Repeat from *, ending rnd with 2 ch, 1 slip st in 3rd of beginning ch. This forms a complete

Rosette, but when working last rnd, this is connected to main part at the same time as given in Finishing.

Border: 1 sc, *skip 3 sts, 10 dc in next st, skip 3 sts, 1 sc in next st, repeat from *.

Tension: 10 spaces and 22 R = 10 cm or 4". Diameter of Rosette = 7 cm or 2¾".

Abbreviations: Ch = chain. Sc = single crochet. Dc = double crochet. St(s) = stitch(es). R = row(s). Rnd(s) = round(s).

Crochet directions

Back: Make 99 (105) ch and work in Basic Pattern — 32 (34) spaces. At each end, increase 1 space in every 8th R 3 times — 38 (40) spaces. *At the same time,* at 5 cm or 2", leave a circular opening (for insertion of flower) by leaving the center 3 spaces unworked and on either side of these, decrease by 1 space in every 2nd R 2 times. To do this, work to division,

turn, work slip st in center of 1st space, continue in pattern to end. In next 2 R, decrease in same way. Work 6 R straight, then increase in every 2nd R at circle edge by 1 space 2 times. Work other side to match, then at end, for the 3 center spaces, make 9 further ch and join up across other sts. Work straight to 14 (15) cm or 5½" (6").

Shape Shoulders: At each end of every R, decrease 1 space 10 (9) times and 2 spaces 1 (2) time(s). *At the same time,* at 17 (18) cm or 6½" (7"), shape for neck by leaving the center 10 spaces unworked and work on each side separately, decreasing 1 space on every 2nd R 2 times.

Right Front: Make 54 (57) ch; work in Basic Pattern — 17 (18) spaces. Keeping front edge straight, increase 1 space in every 10th R 2 times — 19 (20) spaces. *At the same time,* in the 4th R, work the circle as for Back, working 4 spaces, then turn leaving

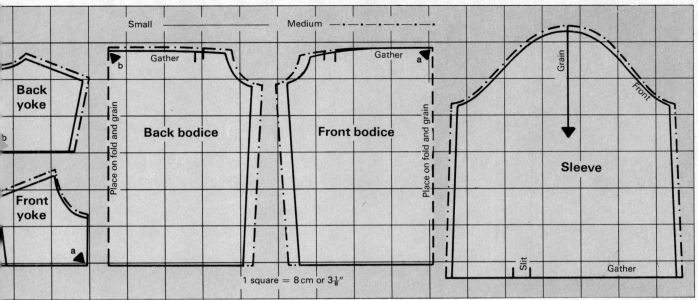

Back yoke

Front yoke

Back bodice

Front bodice

Gather

Gather

Small —————

Medium — · — · —

Place on fold and grain

Place on fold and grain

b

a

Sleeve

Grain

Front

Slit

Gather

1 square = 8 cm or 3⅛"

Enlarge the pattern pieces from the graph pattern given above.

Here is a detail of a rosette. Each is worked separately and crocheted onto the cuffs and yokes.

This is the rosette in the back yoke. The crocheted yoke is sewn onto the fabric blouse with backstitch.

next 3 spaces. After circle is completed, continue straight to 11 (11.5) cm or 4¼" (4½").

Shape Neck: At beginning of every neck edge R, decrease 2 spaces 2 times, then 1 space on every 2nd R 3 times. When piece measures 14 (15) cm or 5½" (6"), shape shoulder as for Back.

Left Front: Work as for Right Front, reversing shapings.

Cuffs: Make 54 ch and work in Basic Pattern – 17 spaces. At 5 cm or 2", increase 1 space on both sides – 19 spaces. *At the same time,* 4 R up work circle as on Back, leaving the center 3 spaces unworked. When Cuff measures 10 cm or 4", fasten off.

Finishing: Make 5 Rosettes and connect in Rnd 5 to the circles of main part. For this, after 5 dc of a shell, withdraw hook from loop, draw loop through the appropriate place in the pattern, then continue to work the shell. Pin out parts and steam

carefully. Join shoulder seams with 1 R of Basic Pattern, connecting loops. Work 1 R of sc around all edges. Now work Border all around neck opening, and around end and sides of cuffs. Twist a cord of 4 strands and thread through holes around neck, just below border.

Making the blouse

Wash the fabric before cutting out, as it may shrink. Enlarge the pattern from the graph. The yoke shape has been added so that you can check the size and shape of the crochet inset.

Cutting out: For seam allowance, add 2 cm (¾") for the hem, 1 cm (⅜") elsewhere. Cut out in single fabric with the front and back below one another, the sleeves with sleeve top against sleeve top.

Sewing: Join the side seams and finish them together close to the stitching line, cutting off the surplus fabric. Turn the hem under twice and

stitch. Finish the yoke edges and press the seam allowance to the inside. Gather the front to 34 cm or 13⅜" (36 cm or 14¼") and the back to 33 cm or 13" (35 cm or 13¾") between the marks.

Finish the armhole edges. Join the sleeve seam and finish the edges. At the sleeve hem, cut in at the marked slit lines and turn under twice. Stitch down by hand or machine. Finish the remaining sleeve hem edge, press under once, and gather to about 19 cm (7½"). Finish the sleeve top and stitch the lower part to back and front bodice. At the upper edge of the sleeve top, press under the seam allowance and gather to 30 cm or 11¾" (31 cm or 12¼"). Finally, sew in the crocheted yoke with backstitch. The yoke fronts meet at center front. The cuffs are sewn on so that the shell edges overlap at sides. Sew 3 buttons on each cuff and button through the pattern.

Hands up!

Pretty gloves are back in fashion, and are the perfect complement to your light, summer wardrobe. Make them in cotton in fresh white or to color co-ordinate with an outfit.

Size: Glove size 7.
Materials Required:

50 gm or 2 oz. Crochet hook 2.
Basic Pattern: Work Foundation — ch Rnd. Rnd 1: *1 sc into ch, 1 ch, skip 3 sts, repeat from * all around, join with a slip st. Rnd 2: 2 ch, *1 sc in each ch loop, 4 ch, repeat from * all around, join with a slip st. Repeat Rnd 2.
Tension: 12 loops and 24 rnds = 10 cm or 4".
Abbreviations: Ch = chain. Sc = single crochet. Dc = double crochet. St(s) = stitch(es). Rnd(s) = round(s).

DIRECTIONS

Right Glove: Make 72 ch and join into a ring with a slip st. Mark end of round with colored thread. Work in Basic Pattern on 18 loops for 7 rnds. In Rnd 8, work pattern as in Diagram between 10th and 11th loops. Now continue to follow Diagram for Back of Hand. *At the same time,* begin increase for Palm in Rnd 9. Work 4 loops then in next loop work 1 sc, 3 ch, 1 sc (1 loop thus increased). Work 2 more increases in the same way in Rnds 13 and 17, *and* increase for Thumb in Rnds 12 and 16 by working increase loop (in same way as Palm increase) in 3rd loop before end of rnd — 26 loops.

Complete Rnd 18, then at end of Rnd 19 leave last 6 loops unworked for Thumb, make 4 ch to count as 1 loop and work in Basic Pattern over 21 loops. Continue straight until 25 rnds from beginning have been worked. Divide for Fingers. Index Finger: Work on last 3 loops of rnd, and first 3 loops of next rnd, turn. Make 3 ch and continue in rnds on these 7 loops for 17 rnds. Draw the center of loops together and fasten off firmly. Divide the 15 remaining loops for 2nd, 3rd, and 4th Fingers — 5 loops for each taking them alternately, 3 from back and 2 from front, then vice versa. 2nd Finger: Make 4 ch between Index and 2nd Fingers and 4 ch between 2nd and 3rd Fingers and work 18 rnds on these 7 loops. Fasten off as before. 3rd Finger: Work to correspond, but work 17 rnds. 4th Finger: Make 4 ch between 3rd and 4th Fingers and work on the 6 loops for 13 rnds. Fasten off. Thumb: Work over the 6 unworked loops and the ch — 7 loops. Work 13 rnds and fasten off.
Cuff Edge: Rnd 1: 3 ch, *1 ch, skip 1 ch of Foundation Rnd, 1 dc on next ch, repeat from * all around, omitting last dc, and join with a slip st. Rnd 2: 1 ch, *(2 sc into each ch space, 1 sc into dc) 3 times, 5 ch, skip 3 dc, repeat from * all around, join with a slip st. Rnd 3: * 1 sc into 3rd sc, skip 3 sc, 3 ch, 1 sc in next sc, skip 3 sc, 12 dc into 5-ch loop, repeat from * all around, join with slip st. Rnd 4: Skip 1 sc and 1 ch, then 1 ch, *1 half dc in ch, 1 ch, (1 dc, 1 ch) in each of 12 dc omitting last 1 ch, repeat from * all around, join with a slip st.
Rnd 5: *1 sc in ch loop, 3 ch, repeat from * all around, join with a slip st and fasten off.
Left Glove: Work to match Right Glove, reversing all shapings.

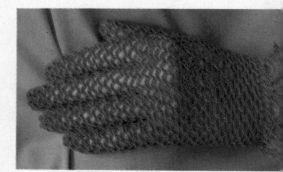

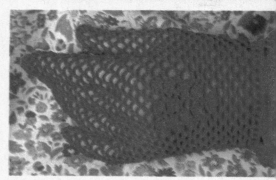

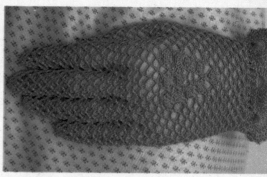

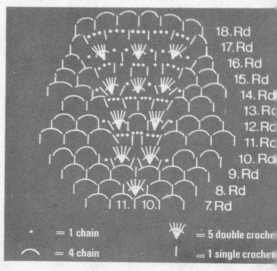

18. Rd
17. Rd
16. Rd
15. Rd
14. Rd
13. Rd
12. Rd
11. Rd
10. Rd
9. Rd
8. Rd
7. Rd

11. 10.

• = 1 chain = 5 double croche
⌒ = 4 chain | = 1 single crochet

Glitter for evening

An evening dress makes you feel pretty and romantic, but you often need something extra around your shoulders when the nights get too chilly. Here are two ideas: a pretty fringed triangular shawl, and a long, long stole in sparkling Lurex.

For Both
Materials Required:

Lurex yarn in quantity and color given in individual directions [20 gm = 128 m or 140 yds]. Crochet hook size C.

Basic Pattern: R 1: 1 sc into 3rd ch from hook, then 1 sc into each st to end, turn with 1 ch. R 2: Sc in sc, turn with 1 ch. R 3: 2 sc, *3 ch, skip 2 sts, 1 sc in next sc (1 loop), repeat from * number of times given in pattern, working 2 sc between each section of loops, ending 2 sc, turn with 1 ch. R 4: 2 sc, 1 ch, *1 sc in loop, 3 ch, repeat from * required number of times, ending each loop section 1 sc in loop, 1 ch, 1 sc and working 2 sc between each section, turn with 1 ch. R 5: 2 sc, *3 ch, 1 sc in loop, repeat from * required number of times, ending each loop section 3 ch, 1 sc, and working 2 sc between each loop section, turn with 1 ch. Repeat R 4 and 5.

Crochet Diagram: The two ends plus one repeat are given for the panels with many circles of single crochet, as well as a single circle motif which is worked in the 9-loop panels.

Tension: About 7 loops and 19 R = 10 cm or 4″.

Abbreviations: St(s) = stitch(es). Ch = chain. Sc = single crochet. R = row(s).

The triangular shawl is in metallic yarn with long fringes to add movement and additional glitter to the total effect. The design is one of stripes and circles.

Triangular Shawl

Size: Width across widest part is about 150 cm or 59". Length from tip to lower edge is about 110 cm or 43".

Materials Required: 320 gm or 12 oz silver.

DIRECTIONS

Make 330 ch and work 2 R of sc as for Basic Pattern — 328 sc. Divide into panels thus: 2 sc, 9 loops of (3 ch, skip 2 sts, 1 sc), 2 sc, 16 loops, 2 sc, 9 loops, 2 sc, 36 loops, 2 sc, 9 loops, 2 sc, 16 loops, 2 sc, 9 loops, 2 sc.

Now work in Basic Pattern in these divisions to end of R 6. In 7th R work single circles of sc in the 2nd and 3rd 9-loop groups, working from the Crochet Diagram. Work in loop pattern and sc as before over remaining sts. Continue thus until the 23rd R has been worked, then work pattern from 1st R of Crochet Diagram and in 7th R work 1 circle in each 9-loop panel, 2 in the 16-loop panel, and 5 in the 36-loop panel. Continue until the 23rd R is worked, then work 2 R of sc as given for R 1 and 2.

Shape point: In next R in the outer edge of each 16-loop panel, decrease 1 loop, then decrease 1 loop alternately in every 2nd then 4th R. *At the same time*, work single circles — as at beginning — in 2nd and 3rd 9-loop panels, working from R 3–23 1 time, then from R 4–23 1 time. Now keeping sc panels, continue in loop pattern, still decreasing 1 loop each end until the 3-sc edges meet. Count the 3 sc as 1 loop for decreasing and continue decreasing until only outer panels remain. Decrease 1 loop each end inside edge sts on every 2nd R until 4 sc remain. Decrease 2 sts 2 times and fasten off.

Finishing: Pin out work,

Patterns show the arrangement of circles on the shawl and stole. The narrow lines = single crochet.

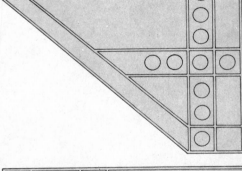

◀ The pattern on the long stole is the same as for the shawl and it also has long fringes.

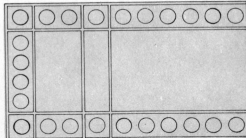

cover with a damp cloth and leave to dry. For fringe, cut 40 cm or 16″ long strands and using 5 strands at a time, knot into every 2nd R or st.

Stole

Size: About 55 cm by 180 cm or 21½″ by 71″.

Materials Required: 320 gm or 12 oz rust.

DIRECTIONS

Make 154 ch and ** work 2 R sc, turning each R with 1 ch – 152 sts. Working in Basic Pattern, divide next R in panels of 2 sc, 9 loops of (3 ch, skip 2 sts, 1 sc), 2 sc, 30 loops, 2 sc, 9 loops, 2 sc, turn with 1 ch. Continue in Basic Pattern and work sc into sc between groups until R 6 has been worked. In next R, begin 1 circle in each of the two 9-loop panels and 4 circles across the 30-loop panel, following Crochet Diagram from R 7–23, then work 2 R of sc as for R 1 and 2. Continue loop pattern over 30-loop panel and work single circles in the 9-loop panel, working from R 3–23 of Crochet Diagram, then from R 4–23. Work 2 more R of sc as before, then divide work into the loop panels once again and work circles in the end panels, following the Crochet Diagram from R 3–23. Work 2 R of sc over all sts **. Divide work into loop panels once more, working a circle in each of the 9-loop panels by working from R 3–23, then repeating from R 4–23 11 times. Now work in reverse from ** to ** to match other end. Fasten off.

Finishing: See Shawl.

Pattern for shawl and stole

1 Crochet-loops pattern: *3 chains, skip 2 single crochets, single crochet into the next single crochet, repeat from *.

2 In following row, 1 chain, *1 single crochet in loop, 3 chains, repeat from the *, ending 1 single crochet, 1 chain.

3 Circles of single crochet: begin with two single crochets into one loop, 1 single crochet into the single crochet, and 2 single crochets into the following loop.

4 In all following rows, increase only 1 single crochet into the adjacent loop on each side until there are 13 stitches. Work 4 rows straight, then decrease as before.

Crochet Diagram for the circles

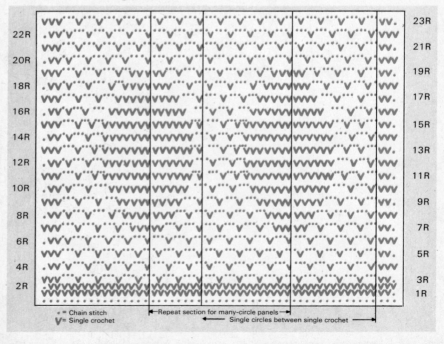

Filet mesh variation

For cool evening breezes

This large three-cornered shawl will drape gracefully around your shoulders to give just the right amount of warmth for a cool evening. The pattern is feminine and the thick, long fringe will swing gently as you move.

Crochet

Size: Across widest side: 180 cm or 72". Short sides: 128 cm or 50½".

Materials Required:

400 gm or 15 oz ecru [50 gm = 155 m or 169 yds]. Crochet hook size E.

Basic Pattern: R 1: 1 dc into 6th ch, *1 ch, skip 1 ch, 1 dc into next st, repeat from * to end, turn with 4 ch. R 2: *1 dc in next dc, then 1 cluster (yarn over hook, hook into ch space and draw loop through, pulling it up to length of a dc 6 times, pass yarn over hook and through all 13 loops on hook, 1 ch), (1 dc on next dc, 1 ch) 3 times, repeat from * to end, finishing 1 dc, 1 ch, 1 dc after last cluster, turn with 4 ch. R 3: *1 dc on next dc, 1 ch. Repeat from * ending 1 dc into 3rd of 4 ch, turn with 4 ch. Repeat R 2 and R 3 for the pattern, but alternate the clusters as shown in photograph.

Tension: 18 sts and 9 R = 10 cm or 4".

Abbreviations: St(s) = stitch(es). R = row(s). Sc = single crochet. Dc = double crochet. Tr = treble stitch.

DIRECTIONS

Begin at one short side, working straight at left side and decreasing on right side for long diagonal.

Make 234 ch and work in Basic Pattern, but decrease at end of R 2 by working to dc after last cluster, yarn over, hook into dc, draw up loop (2 loops on hook), 1 tr into turning ch, drawing through last 3 loops on hook, turn with 4 ch. In next R, begin by working a dc into next dc.

Decrease in this way at end of every cluster R until 1 space remains. Turn and work in sc all around outer edges. Fasten off.

Finishing: Press lightly. Cut yarn into 35 cm or 13¾" lengths and make a knotted fringe along both short side edges, positioned in center spaces between clusters.

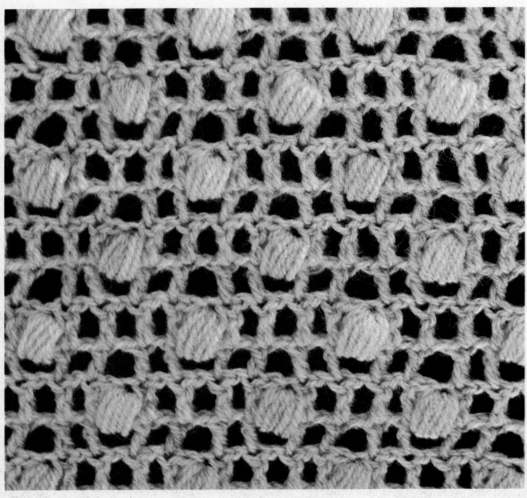

◄ Clusters are worked in a staggered pattern to create an interesting variation to the standard filet mesh design.

Cluster stitch in filet mesh

The cluster stitch is made by working several loops into a space, then drawing the yarn through all of the loops. They are always worked from the wrong side and produce a knob in relief on the right side of the piece.

Cluster stitch

1 To begin the cluster stitch, pass the hook under the yarn, then insert the hook into the space below.

2 Pass the hook under the yarn. Draw it through the space up to the height of the double crochet.

3 Repeat steps 1 and 2 for required number of times, keeping all loops on the hook.

4 Pass the hook under the yarn and draw the yarn through the loops on the hook.

5 Finish the cluster with a chain stitch, then continue across the row.

Decreasing one space

1 Work to last two double crochets. Work double crochet, but leave last two loops on hook; work a treble, then draw yarn through all loops.

2 Turn the work with four chain stitches and begin the next row with a double crochet into the next double crochet. Continue to work across row.

Ring strips

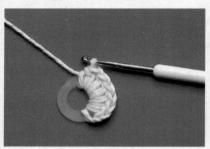

1 To crochet into the ring, attach the yarn to the ring, make 1 sc and 1 ch, then make as many hdc around the ring as stated, join with a slip st to 1 ch.

2 In the 2nd rnd, work sc in the horizontal threads at back of sts. For 2nd and all other rings, connect the last 3 sts with the first 3 sts of previous ring.

3 When all rings have been connected, then the upper and lower edges are straightened with a crochet border. For this, *work 5 sc, beginning in the 3rd st of the 3 connecting sts . . .

4 . . . then to get the straight edge, work 1 hdc and 1 dc in next 2 sts, 1 tr between rings, then 1 hdc and 1 dc in next 2 sts. Repeat from * all around, joining each rnd with a slip st.

Crab stitch

1 For crab st, single crochet sts are worked from left to right. For the flat R of crab sts used in the bag on the right, * 1 ch, skip 1 st, then insert hook into next st . . .

2 Take hook around the yarn from left to right and draw out loop, take hook around the yarn again in the same way, and loop off both loops. Repeat from *.

The texture of the bag has a woven look that gives it a craftsman touch. Plastic curtain rings are crocheted together to create an extra-durable bag. The straps are long enough to sling over the shoulder for maximum convenience.

Keep it around

City-dwellers need not despair! This long holdall will see you through a busy day in town without letting you down. It's strong enough to accommodate heavy loads and yet stylish enough to take with you anywhere.

Size: Circumference is 70 cm or 27½", height is 48 cm or 19".

Materials Required:

Jute: 600 m or 656 yds natural, 100 m or 109 yds dark brown. Crochet hook size D. 70 plastic curtain rings, 2.5 cm or 1" in diameter.

Abbreviations: Ch = chain. Sc = single crochet. Dc = double crochet. St(s) = stitch(es). Rnd(s) = round(s). Hdc = half double crochet. Tr = treble.

DIRECTIONS

Bag Base: Using natural, make 4 ch and join into a ring with a slip st (join all rnds with a slip st). Rnd 1: 7 sc in ring. Rnd 2: 2 sc in each sc — 14 sc. Rnd 3: (1 sc in sc, 2 sc in next sc) all around — 21 sc. Rnd 4: (2 sc, 2 sc in next sc) all around — 28 sc.
Continue in this way until Rnd 20 is completed — 140 sc. Fasten off.

Bag Strips: For each strip, you need 14 curtain rings. Rnd 1: With natural, join to ring and work 1 sc, 1 ch, then 24 hdc in ring, join with a slip st to ch. Rnd 2: 1 ch, then work 24 sc, but work in the cross-thread that is behind the ch at top of hdc, thus giving a ch effect all around.
Repeat Rnds 1 and 2, joining them to each other in the 2nd rnd. For this, work 21 sc as given, then connect last 3 sc with first 3 sc of previous ring (see How-to). Connect the 14th ring to 1st ring at corresponding place.
Now, still working into the horizontal thread as before, join yarn to the 3rd st of the 3 connecting sts of 1st ring, *work 5 sc along top of ring, then 1 hdc in next st, 1 dc in next st, 1 tr between ring (see How-to), 1 dc in corresponding st of next ring, 1 hdc in next st. Repeat from * to end of rnd and join with a slip st.
Work around the lower edge of strip in same way. Work 5 strips in all.

Finishing: Using brown, join base and strips together on wrong side with sc, inserting hook into the thread that now faces you. When all strips have been joined, work 1 rnd of crab stitch from left to right thus: *1 ch, skip 1 st, 1 crab sc st to left, repeat from * all around, join with a slip st, and fasten off.
Make 2 twisted cords with 5 threads each about 80 cm or 32" long. Draw through 1st rnd of holes in top strip.

Border with clusters

How to work the shawl border. R 1–3 are in white.

R 1: 4 ch for turn, 1 dc each in 1st dc, ch, and next dc, *skip 1 st, 1 ch, 1 dc in each of the next 3 sts, repeat from *, but work 5 dc in corner dc, and end the R after last 3 dc with 1 ch and 1 dc in 3rd of the turning ch.

1 R 2: 4 ch for the turn, *1 tr, 5 ch, 1 tr in next ch space, 1 cluster of 5 half-finished tr looped off together in next ch space, repeat from * to last ch space before corner.

2 Work corner thus: 1 tr, 5 ch, 1 tr in ch space, 1 cluster of 5 half-finished tr looped off together in corner dc, then work along other side to match, ending R with 1 tr, 5 ch, 1 tr in last ch space and 1 tr into 3rd of turning ch. R 3: work 4 ch to turn, 2 tr into 1st tr, continue to work as for R 2 . . . . . .

3 . . . . . . working the tr in the center of the 5 ch sts, and clusters on the clusters. The resulting pattern is shown above.

4 At corner, work 1 cluster, 5 ch, 1 cluster, then work to end of R with 2 tr in last tr and 1 tr in the 4th turning ch. R 4: (green) Work 1 dc on each st with 5 dc at corner. R 5: (green) 3 ch for turn, 1 dc in last dc, 2 ch, 1 dc in 3rd dc, *skip 2 sts, 2 ch, 1 dc in following 3rd st, repeat from * to corner, working (2 ch, 1 dc) 3 times in corner st, then work to end, matching ends with 1 dc taking place of 3 ch. R 6: (green) Turn with 5 ch, 1 dc in 2nd dc, *2 ch, 1 dc in next dc, repeat from * to corner, working this as for R 5, then work to end, matching ends with 2 ch, 1 dc in place of 5 ch. R 7: (navy) 1 dc in each st with 5 dc in corner st. R 8: (white) Repeat R 5.

make it bold

The stripes are bold, the pattern simple. To soften the effect, a decorative border and long tassels have been added.

Materials Required:

200 gm or 8 oz green, 120 gm or 5 oz blue, 80 gm or 3 oz white, 40 gm or 2 oz navy [40 gm = 124 m or 135 yds]. Crochet hook size D.

Basic Pattern: R 1: (blue) Make 4 ch, turn, and in 1st of these ch work (1 ch, 1 dc) 4 times. R 2: (blue) 3 ch for turn, then 1 ch and 1 dc in 1st dc, 1 ch and 1 dc in 2nd dc, (1 ch and 1 dc in 3rd dc) 3 times for corner, 1 ch and 1 dc in 4th dc, (1 ch and 1 dc) 2 times in 3rd of turning ch. R 3: (blue) 3 ch for turn, then 1 ch and 1 dc in 1st dc, (1 ch and 1 dc) in all dc to corner dc, (1 ch, 1 dc) 3 times in corner dc, then 1 ch, 1 dc in dc to end, working (1 ch, 1 dc) 2 times in 3rd of turning ch. R 4–10: (blue) R 3. R 11–13: (white) 3 ch for turn, 2 dc in 1st dc, work 1 dc in each st to corner dc, 5 dc in corner dc, in dc in each remaining st, ending 3 dc in 3rd of turning ch. R 14–20: (green) Repeat R 3, but work in alternate dc to keep continuity of blocks. R 21: (white) In dc as for R 11. R 22 and 23: (navy) Repeat R 14. R 24: (white) In dc as for R 11. Repeat R 4–24 1 more time. R 46–55: (blue) Repeat R 14.

Tension: 26 sts and 12 R = 10 cm or 4".

Abbreviations: Ch = chain. Sc = single crochet. Dc = double crochet. Tr = treble. St(s) = stitch(es). R = row(s).

DIRECTIONS

Work shawl as given in Basic Pattern, then work the 8 R of border given in the How-to. Using green, finish upper edge with 1 R sc. For fringe: knot 4 24 cm or 9½" lengths into each ch space of edge.

Style 1: To begin, there is an overblouse in sizes A and C. With the boat-shaped neckline, which crosses over the shoulders, there are no fastenings to worry about. Elastic casings gather in the cuffs and waist, and there is a neat patch pocket on the front.

Style 2: Next, a blouson-style shirt in sizes B and D. It is easy to sew because the sleeves are cut in one with the main body. It has elastic at the waist and wrists and the front and back are pleated onto the yoke. The pockets are stitched diagonally onto the fronts and bound.

Tops for sports

Whether you want separates for sporting or simply casual wear, this superb collection will win your praise. The styles have a comfortable cut, fashion detailing, and mix-and-match potential. All the styles can be made from Pattern Sheet 65.

Style 3: Use the same pattern as for Style 2, but cut this style to hip length. The hem is rounded off into side slits and there is an inverted pleat down the center back. The tie belt turns the overblouse into a long jacket which will be an indispensable part of your wardrobe.

◀ Style 1: Here you can see the crossed shoulders which eliminate the need for fastenings. Simply slip it on.

◀ Style 2: This is the back view of the casual overblouse. Note that the back is pleated onto the yoke. Note the bias cut of the collar fabric.

Style 3: The front view of the jacket shows the smart collar rising directly from the front facing. The pockets sport unusual, ▼ decorative tabs.

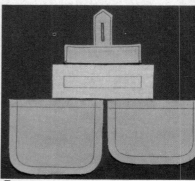

1 All the pattern pieces for this pocket style are shown above. At the very top is the tab, in the center is the interfacing, on the lower left is the upper pocket lining and on the lower right is the lower pocket lining. For the flap, cut two strips 10 cm (4″) long by 1.5 cm ($\frac{5}{8}$″) wide, plus seam allowances of 1 cm ($\frac{3}{8}$″) on the upper edge and 0.5 cm ($\frac{1}{4}$″) on the other three sides. To reinforce the opening, cut a strip of iron-on interfacing to measure 13 cm (5″) long by 4.5 cm ($1\frac{5}{8}$″) wide. Iron the interfacing strip to the fabric. Stitch and turn the tab, make a buttonhole where indicated, then top-stitch. Stitch and turn the flap, catching in the tab. Top-stitch the flap.

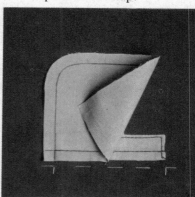

2 Pin the flap along the upper basting line, right sides facing and with the tab facing upward. Baste if necessary, then stitch in place. Pin the upper lining on top of it as shown in the photograph above and stitch along the seamline, right sides facing. Make sure that you stitch right into the corners, and that you fasten off the thread ends firmly.

Pocket with tab fastening

This pocket tab is not intended to be particularly practical, but is often used for a decorative effect. Though not difficult, it does require patience and care. Do not use thick fabric as this will only complicate matters. To clarify the various stages of working, we have used two different fabric colors, though you would use only one.

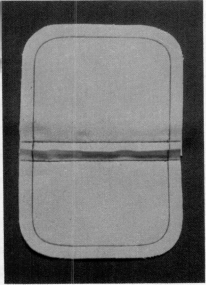

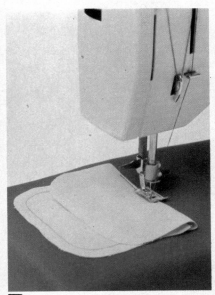

3 Stitch the lower pocket lining to the lower basting line, right sides facing, as shown above. Stitch carefully into the corners as before, and secure the ends of the threads neatly in the same way as for the upper pocket lining.

5 To prevent the seam at the upper edge of the lower pocket lining from splitting during wear, stitch down along the seam allowance as shown above. Avoid catching the triangles formed at the ends into the stitching.

6 Place the upper and lower pocket linings together and pin the two layers around the outer edge, pushing in the pins at right angles as shown above. Stitch around the marked seamline, then finish the seam allowances together.

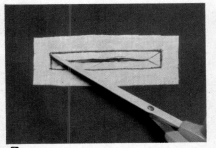

4 Cut along the center line between the two rows of stitching. Cut through the outer fabric only, not the lining. Snip diagonally into the four corners. Work slowly and carefully.

7 Sew a button onto the right side of the front where marked and button down the tab. The completed pocket tab should look as beautifully and professionally finished as it does in the photograph above.

Style 1

Style 2

Style 4

Style 3

Cool customer

Red and white is the most stunning color combination for summer, so follow our lead and make this collection of separates. All styles are in sizes B and D on Pattern Sheet 66.

Style 1: This is a long shirt which doubles as a jacket. It's gathered onto a yoke at front and back and has short sleeves with turn-back cuffs and buttoned tabs.

Other details include patch pockets and a top-stitched buttonband.

Style 2: Add these smart pants and you have a suit. The pants are cut straight and have unpressed pleats in the front.

Style 3: You can also make bermuda shorts. They have an elastic casing at the waist and the legs have turn-ups.

Style 6

Style 4

Styles 4 and 5

Style 4: Extend your wardrobe with this useful shirt. Above left you can see it with bermuda shorts and tied at the midriff for a casual look. On this page it is teamed with a matching skirt to look like a dress. It has patch pockets and wide sleeves with turn-back cuffs. The front and back are gathered onto the yoke and all the seams are top-stitched.

Style 5: The skirt is flared and has an inverted pleat down the front. It has large patch pockets and is gathered slightly onto the waistband.

Style 6: Top the lot with a neat little hat cut on the bias. Make a contrasting band and top-stitch all around to finish.

Making a summer hat

For this hat you will need six sections in both fabric and iron-on woven interfacing. Note the brim is cut out twice. All the pieces should be cut on the bias for a better fit. Add seam allowances of 1 cm ($\frac{3}{8}''$) on the lower edge of the crown and 0.5 cm ($\frac{1}{4}''$) on all other edges. We have used two fabrics for clarity.

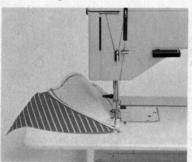

1 Crown: Iron the interfacings to the 6 crown sections, then sew these together in 2 sets of 3 sections. Stitch from the lower edge toward the point, but not into the seam allowance. Secure the ends firmly, making sure that you do not stitch into any of the seam allowances of the other sections.

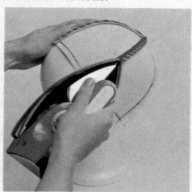

2 Press the seams of each 3-section part open carefully over a curved surface such as a tailor's pressing ham. If you intend to make several hats, it might be a good idea to buy a wig stand, either in wood or in the cheaper polystyrene. If the stand is in polystyrene, take care not to touch the surface with the iron because it will melt.

3 On the apex of the crown, cut away the ends of the seam allowances diagonally to prevent a build up of fabric.

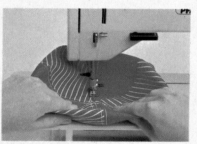

4 Stitch the 2 3-section parts together. Press open the seams, then trim away the seam allowances at the top of the crown. Top-stitch the seams.

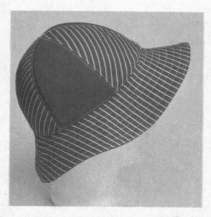

5 Baste along the seamline at the lower edge of the crown.
Brim: Stitch the center back seams of both layers separately, then with right sides facing, stitch both together around the outer edge and turn to the right side. Baste the stitched edge carefully, then baste along the open edge to hold the two layers securely in place. Top-stitch the brim at regular intervals right up to this line of basting to give the brim added firmness. Take out the basting, and turn the seam allowances to the inside. Place the lower edge of the crown between the brim edges and pin in place all around. Stitch the brim to the crown from the right side.

6 The finished hat will look like this. If you have a smaller head size than the one given on the pattern, stitch inside the marked seamlines of the 6 sections. If your head size is larger, stitch outside the marked seamlines. This will mean that the brim will be slightly wider or narrower at the back when the brim and crown are stitched together. Keep your hat on the wig stand when it is not being worn.

Style 7

Style 7

Style 7: To give style and flair to the whole collection, we've added a pair of overalls. The front bands and pocket flaps are studded with shiny snaps and the waist and wrists are drawn in with elastic. There are also deep pockets in the legs. All the detailing has double top-stitching. Above, you can see them from the back. Note that the yoke fabric has been cut on the bias, but the main body has been cut along the stripes for a more flattering and slimming effect.

Style 1

67

Cotton on to it

Here is a selection of easy-to-sew and easy-care cotton styles for summer. Choose fresh colors in stripes, checks, and plaids.

Style 1: Start with this cool little dress which can be made in sizes C and E from Pattern Sheet 67. Narrow and straight, it is particularly *slimming in effect if the stripes are worked vertically. Long side slits in the slim skirt allow for freedom of movement. The pockets are set into the side seams and the collar is open and stylish. Note that the neck and sleeve bands are cut crosswise for contrast.

Style 2: Given in sizes B and D, this useful style has a figure-flattering close-fitting bodice. The short sleeves are cut-in-one with the bodice and have under-arm gussets. The skirt is gathered into the waist and there is a buttoned fastening down the front. There are also patch pockets on the bodice and two more pockets in the side seams.

Style 3: Check this smart dress in sizes C and E. It's cut straight, has short sleeves cut-in-one with the bodice, and a deep, deep neck line. Sleeves, pockets, and the neck are banded in plain fabric for maximum effect. Add patch pockets to the front of the skirt, insert a zipper into the back, then complete the look with a belt.

Style 2

Style 3

Style 1: This detail shows the skirt of the straight dress on the previous page. Here you can see how the stripes meet along the side seam. Note that the depth of the side slit will allow you to stride through the summer with the greatest of ease.

Style 2: The most unusual feature of the dress is the gusset in each sleeve. This allows movement and gives the garment flair and dash. The How-to on the right shows the method for inserting such a gusset.

Inserting a sleeve gusset

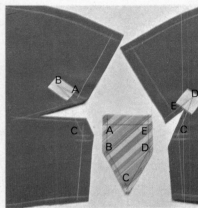

1 Here are the various patter pieces. On the left is the fron on the right the back. The stripe gusset is in the middle. The gusse placement lines must be reinforce Press iron-on interfacings over th points on the wrong side of th fabric. On the front piece it approximately 5 cm (2″) long by cm (1¼″) wide; on the back, 4 c (1½″) square. Stitch along th marked lines from the interfacin side. Finish the gusset edges exce for the sleeve hem edge as show above.

2 Stitch the dart, working onl as far as the center of the tw gusset placement lines. Finish th cut edges and press downwar so the dart will not be obvious.

Where a garment incorporates a kimono-type sleeve into the bodice, a gusset is usually inserted under the arm to improve the fit and allow room for movement. The gusset is striped for clarity.

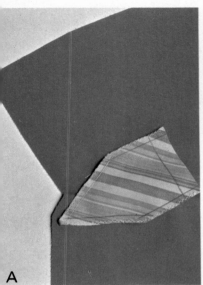

A

4 Either pin or baste the gusset along the line marked A–B, right sides facing, then stitch into place. (Mark the letters on the fabric with chalk so that you know exactly where you are.) Stitch right into the point to prevent it from tearing. Work carefully and precisely. Secure the ends of the threads, then press the seams toward the gusset.

6 Stitch along line A–D and press seam toward gusset. The illustration above shows the inserted gusset which extends from the sleeve hem down into the side seam.

B

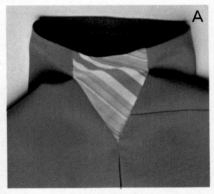

A

3 Photograph A: Stitch the gusset along the line marked C–B, right sides facing. Secure the thread ends carefully.
Photograph B: From the wrong side, stitch along the stitching line just made. Cut between the gusset placement lines, up to the point. Take great care not to cut into the stitching or the gusset.

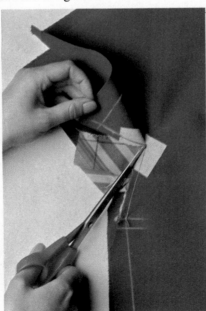

5 The gusset is now attached to the back. Stitch the gusset along line C–D, then secure the ends carefully as before. Cut along the center of the fabric between the two gusset placement lines, up to the point as shown left in photograph and step 3B.

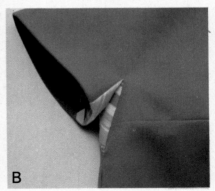

B

7 Now join the side seam immediately below point C. Then join the shoulder seams and finish all cut edges. Finally, turn up and sew the sleeve hem. Photograph A shows the finished gusset from underneath the arm, Photograph B from the front.

Style 1

Style 2

Illustrated Sewing

68

Flatter yourself

Choose two colors such as black and lavender for dramatic effect, then repeat them in different patterned and plain fabrics for a blouse, pleated skirt, dress, and overblouse. All the styles shown here are given on Pattern Sheet 68.

Style 1: The pretty blouse in lilac poplin is wide and roomy. The stitched pleats are released below a stitched band set in the front and the collar extends up from the open neck. The full sleeves are gathered into wide cuffs and all of the detailing is set off by top-stitching. The pattern is for sizes B and D.

Style 2: To team with the blouse, we've created a pleated skirt with some unusual features. There is a deep hip yoke that fastens at the side by means of loops and buttons, a wide waistband, and long ties to wind around your waist time and time again. The skirt is also given in sizes B and D.

Style 3 is a dress for the young at heart. The bodice is tight fitting and the skirt is gathered onto it with small pleats, a feature repeated on the top of the sleeves. Note the square neck and the top-stitched pleats on the bodice. The dress is given in sizes A and C.

Style 3

Style 1

Style 3

Hip yoke with loop fastenings

A

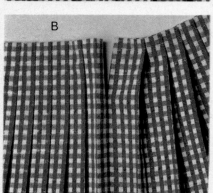

B

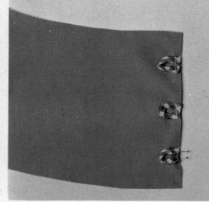

A

B

1 Before beginning to work the loops, press the pleats as instructed, then baste them down along the upper edge. Check that any seams lie hidden inside the pleats. When pleated, the fold line of a pleat lies on the right side at the pleat placement line, forming an overlap and underlap.

The facings at the skirt opening are cut in one with the skirt with seam allowances of 1 cm ($\frac{3}{8}$″) (see Photograph A). Stitch the seam from the hem edge to the bottom of the opening, then press open the seam. Press under the seam allowances at the edges of the skirt opening. Finish all raw edges with zigzag stitching as shown above. Photograph B shows the seam and opening from the right side. The seam is on the inside fold of a pleat and will be completely invisible.

2 The size of the button loops will be determined by the size of the buttons. This style has three loops, each 6 cm (2$\frac{1}{2}$″) long because the circumference of the buttons is 1.7 cm ($\frac{5}{8}$″). Cut them in a single strip 18 cm (7″) long and 2 cm ($\frac{3}{4}$″) wide. If using a thicker fabric, do not turn the strip, but fold the cut edges to the center, fold in half along the center, and stitch close to the edge. Cut the strip into three equal lengths for the loops. Pin them on the right side of the overlap hip yoke, then stitch in place along the seam allowance.

3 Finish the outer edge of the yoke facing and baste it to the overlap yoke, right sides together. Stitch along the seamline, catching in the button loops. Press open the seam allowances.

4 Stitch the darts, then stitch and finish the side seam of the yoke. Pin the yoke to the skirt at the pleated edge, then stitch all around. Photograph A shows the overlap edge with the loops inserted in the facing seam. Photograph B shows the underlap edge. Note edges of skirt yoke facings meet.

5 Press the seam allowance upward where the yoke is joined to the skirt, then finish the edges together. Press under the overlap facing along the seam; press the cut-in-one underlap facing along the marked line. Top-stitch the width of the presser foot from the edge to look as above.

6 Pin the overlap over the underlap, then mark the positions for the buttons. The button placement depends on the shape of the loops. You will find that the flatter the loop, the nearer the edge your button will be. Sew on the buttons. Finally, to prevent the opening from gaping, sew a hook and eye at the base of the yoke.

Style 4

Style 4: This overblouse is quick and easy to make but is in an unusual and original enough design to make it interesting. The neck line is small and round, there are small cap sleeves cut in one with the blouse, and the blouse itself is cut short and straight. The zipper opening is in the back seam. Make it in a quilted print fabric and wear it over plain blouses or T-shirts. Alternatively, choose another co-ordinating print and wear both together. The pattern is in sizes C and E.

Cut the cost

Break away from the traditional three-piece suite by actually making your own sitting room furniture at half the cost. It's fun, practical and very comfortable.

For the cover fabric, we chose a strong, washable cotton velvet — plain and patterned. The inner cushions are made of unbleached cotton filled with kapok. Some of them have a quilted design on the front.

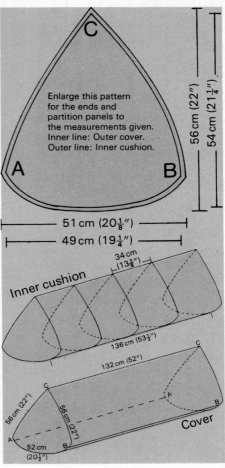

Enlarge this pattern
for the ends and
partition panels to
the measurements given.
Inner line: Outer cover.
Outer line: Inner cushion.

C

A   B

56 cm (22")
54 cm (21¼")

51 cm (20⅛")
49 cm (19¼")

34 cm
(13⅜")

Inner cushion

136 cm (53½")

132 cm (52")

C

56 cm (22")

56 cm (22")

A

B

A

B

52 cm
(20½")

Cover

1 Back and side bolsters

Materials Required (for each):
Inner Cushion: 3.50 m (3⅞ yds),
140 cm (54") wide. Cover fabric:
5 m (5½ yds), 70 cm (27") wide.
Zipper: 100 cm (40") long. Kapok:
7 kg (15 lbs).

Inner cushion: This is made larger
in circumference as well as in length,
so that the cover is well plumped
out. It consists of 4 compartments,
each 34 cm (13⅜") long.

Cutting out: Cut out 5 tear-shaped
pieces (following outer line) and 4
rectangles 169 cm x 34 cm (66½" x
13⅜") plus 1 cm (⅜") all around for
seam allowance. Make sure the long
sides of the rectangles fit exactly
around the circumference of the
tear-shaped pieces before cutting
them out accurately.

Sewing: Finish the 4 rectangles at
the narrow edges. Stitch each
rectangle to the next around the
long sides, catching in a tear-shaped
piece between them as a partition as
follows: Beginning at point C, first
pin the 3 seam allowances together.
Then stitch and finish all 3 seams
together. At the beginning and end

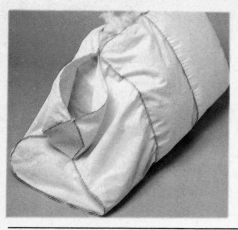

of the bolster, stitch on a tear-shaped piece. You then have an inner cover with 4 compartments (only 3 shown on our photograph on the left) which are open at the top. Stuff these as firmly as possible with kapok. Since kapok clings to fabric, it is advisable to do this job in a room such as the kitchen where there is no carpet or upholstery. Pin up the compartments at once and then sew together by hand.

Cover: Cut out 2 tear-shaped pieces (following inner line) plus 1 cm ($\frac{3}{8}$").

seam allowance. Cut 3 rectangula pieces each 132 cm (52") long, 2 which are 56 cm (22") wide and of which is 52 cm (20½") wide plu seam allowance (see diagram o previous page).

Sewing: First stitch seam B – B right sides facing, for 16 cm (6" from each end. Stitch the zipper i seam opening. Then join seams – A and C – C. Stitch a tear-shape piece at each end. Press the seams turn, and draw cover over the inne cushion.

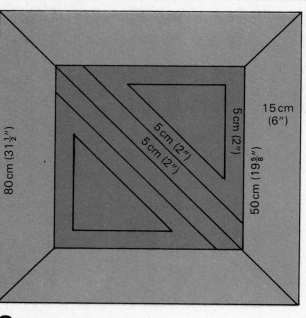

▶ The pale green areas indicate the floral fabric: the dark green areas indicate the plain fabric. Enlarge the pattern to the measurements given.

15 cm (6")

5 cm (2")

5 cm (2")

5 cm (2")

80 cm (31½")

50 cm (19⅝")

Lightly draw in the lines shown i the diagram with the end of a piec of soap. Soap is used on velve because the lines can easily b

removed later with a damp cloth Baste the interlining to the wrong side under the area to be quilted (the demonstration photograph shows the technique on a different cushion) From the right side, stitch along the lines with a matching thread (fo clarity, we used a lighter thread) Also stitch again along the seam lines around the square inset. Cut of the interlining up to the seamlines Place the front and back of the cushion together, right sides facing and stitch one side together 10 cm (3¾") from each end. From the righ side, stitch in the zipper invisibly Then stitch the remaining 3 sides together.

Press the seams open. Turn to the right side and pull cover over inner cushion.

2 Large square cushion

Materials Required for each:
Unbleached cotton: 1.65 m (1⅞ yds), 140 cm (54") wide. Plain fabric: 2.80 m (3⅛ yds), 70 cm (27") wide. Patterned fabric: 0.70 m (¾ yd), 90 cm (36") wide. Batting or wadding for interlining: 0.60 m (⅝ yd), 90 cm (36") wide. Zipper: 60 cm (24") long. Kapok: 2.5 kg (5½ lbs).

Inner cushion: Cutting out: Cut 2 pieces 80 cm (31½") square plus 1 cm (⅜") seam allowance all around. Sewing: Stitch the pieces together, leaving about 20 cm (8") open. Turn and fill firmly with kapok. Sew up the opening by hand.

Cover: For the back, cut out 2 pieces each 40 cm x 80 cm (15¾" x 31½") plus 1 cm (⅜") seam allowance all around. For the front, cut a 50 cm (19⅝") square plus 1 cm (⅜") seam allowance all around. From the patterned fabric, cut 4 pieces as shown in the diagram with 1 cm (⅜") all around for the seam allowance.

From the interlining, cut a 52 cm (20½") square.

Sewing: First stitch the 2 back pieces together along one long side, right sides facing, and press the seam open. Then join the 4 patterned pieces along the diagonal edges, stitching only up to the seam

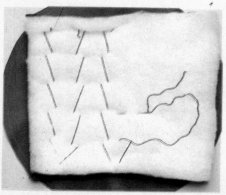

allowance at the inner edges. Press the seams open. Stitch in the square and press these seams open as well. Then top-stitch the front as follows:

Cushions 3, 4, 5, 6, 7, 8, 9

Make these cushions, using the instructions for Cushion 2. Cut out according to the measurements given in the diagrams. The back of each cushion is cut from plain fabric.

Note: The two round cushions should be stuffed very firmly. The backs are each cut out in 2 halves, with the zipper inserted in this seam. We have not given any fabric requirements for the smaller cushions because you can make use of remnants for them. These cushions need not be stuffed quite as firmly as the large cushions.

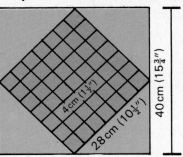

5 Square cushion with patterned corners

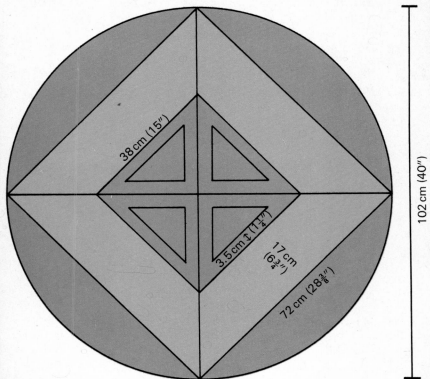

3 Round cushion with square inset

Materials Required: Inner cushion: 2.10 m (2¼ yds), 140 cm (54") wide. Plain fabric: 2.80 m (3⅛ yds), 70 cm (27") wide. Patterned fabric: 0.75 m (⅞ yd), 90 cm (36") wide. Batting or wadding: 1.50 m (1⅝ yds), 90 cm (36") wide. Kapok: 3 kg (6½ lbs). Zipper: 80 cm (32") long.

6 Rectangular cushion with diagonal stripes

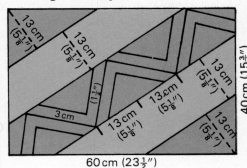

7 Rectangular cushion in patterned fabric

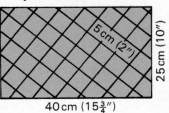

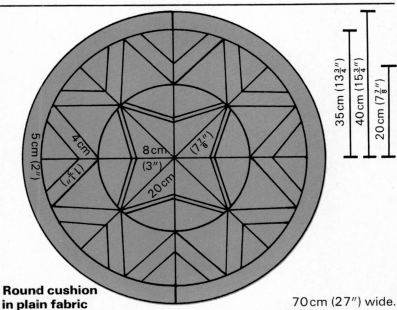

4 Round cushion in plain fabric

Materials Required: Inner cushion: 1.50 m (1⅝ yds), 140 cm (54") wide. Plain fabric: 2.30 m (2½ yds), 70 cm (27") wide. Batting or wadding: 1.65 m (1⅞ yds), 90 cm (36") wide. Zipper: 60 cm (24"). Kapok: 2 kg (4½ lbs).

8 Square cushion in plain fabric

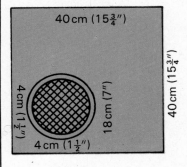

9 Round cushion with square inset

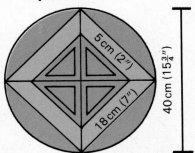

2123

Sunray quilt

Size: 1.55 m x 2.08 m (61" x 82").

Materials Required: Furnishing or upholstery fabric: 5.50 m (6 yds), 122 cm (48") wide in red; 1.45 m (1⅝ yds), 122 cm (48") wide in old rose; 1 m (1⅛ yds), 122 cm (48") wide in pale pink. Taffeta lining: 5.40 m (5⅞ yds), 140 cm (54") wide. Batting or wadding interlining: 6.70 m (7⅜ yds), 145 cm (58") wide.

Making the bedspread

Cut out pieces according to measurements on diagram plus seam allowances.

Add 2 cm (¾") seam allowance on outside edges of Part 4 and seamline of overhang. Add 8 cm (3") at overhang sides and 3 cm (1¼") at hem; elsewhere, add 1 cm (⅜"). Part 2 has center seams on the long sides, Part 3 on all 4 sides. Enlarge the quilting design

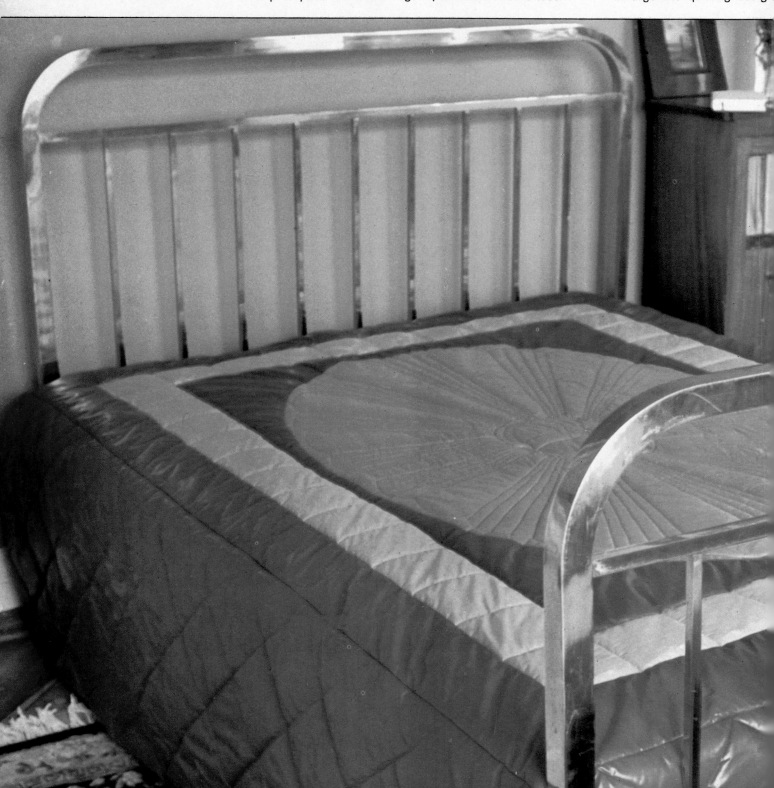

from the graph pattern and transfer onto the oval fabric with white dressmaker's carbon paper and a tracing wheel. Join the small seams of Part 2 and stitch this section around the oval, right sides facing. Baste interlining (with an extra 1 cm ($\frac{3}{8}$") all around) firmly

Our elegant chintz quilt has an overhang on both sides and at the foot. If you wish to make the quilt for a day bed, add another flap to the overhang to cover the head end.

under the oval. Top-stitch as follows: first stitch the center parallel lines, then the semi-circles, then the scallops and finally the rays (always working from the center outward). Take care that the fabric does not drag when working on the bias.

Join the 4 center seams of Part 3, then join the Part 3 strips to the Part 4 strips and press the seams open. Then join the diagonal corner seams. On Part 3, draw in the quilting lines 13 cm (5$\frac{1}{8}$") apart, including the center seams. Join Parts 2 and 3.

Cut 2 interlining pieces 80 cm x 212 cm (31$\frac{1}{2}$" x 83$\frac{1}{2}$") and baste firmly under the whole quilt. Stitch through all connecting seams of Parts 1–4, beginning at the oval. Finally, stitch along the quilting lines of Part 3, always working from the center out as you stitch. Now cut away the second layer of interlining just inside the center oval as this area has already been quilted. At the outer edges, finish the fabric and the interlining together.

Draw in the quilting lines lightly on the overhang with tailor's chalk, baste interlining firmly onto the back, and top-stitch the lines. Turn in the side edges and hem of the overhang and sew by hand. Finish the fabric and interlining together along the seamlines. Stitch the overhang to the quilt. Cut the lining to the quilt measurements (piecing where necessary) plus 2 cm ($\frac{3}{4}$") seam allowance. Pin lining to back and stitch along the seamlines. Slip-stitch to the edges and hems.

Quilting pattern: ▶ **First enlarge the $\frac{1}{4}$ oval given, then draw the quarter next to it as a mirror image. Draw the opposite half to match.**

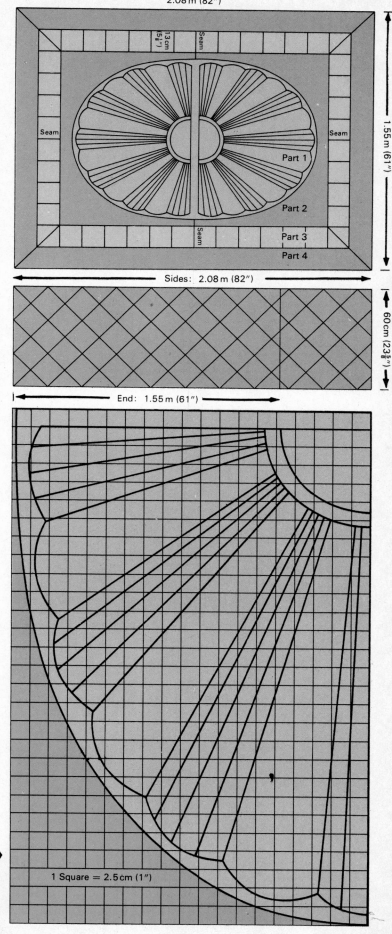

2.08 m (82")

13 cm (5$\frac{1}{8}$")

Seam

Seam

Seam

Part 1

Part 2

Seam

Part 3

Part 4

1.55 m (61")

Sides: 2.08 m (82")

60 cm (23$\frac{5}{8}$")

End: 1.55 m (61")

1 Square = 2.5 cm (1")

Our young model has played
with Floppy for hours.
After all, you can make up
so many games with him –
and use him as a pillow
when you're tired !

Introducing a new friend.....

May I introduce myself: I'm Floppy, the softest, furriest, and friendliest polar bear in the whole world and I can't wait to meet you. I'm always ready for a game, so please cuddle me, carry me, sit on me, or play with me — I never get tired of having fun. My coat is fake-fur fabric and my soft stuffing makes me nice to hold and hug. Let's be playmates!

Materials Required: White fake-fur fabric: 1.10 m (1¼ yd), 140 cm (54″) wide. Remnant of black fake-fur fabric or felt for paws and nose. Kapok for stuffing: about 600 gm (22 oz). 2 eyes.

Cutting out: Enlarge the pattern pieces from the graph onto large sheets of tissue paper, adding seam allowances of 1 cm (⅜″) on all pieces. Place the pieces on wrong side of single fabric and cut out. Half of front body is given; cut out the whole shape in one piece. Cut out the back body, side head, side snout, tail, and paws twice. Cut the ears 4 times. The remaining pieces are cut out once. Remember to cut the nose and paws from black fabric.

Sewing: Stroke the pile away from the seam before pinning and stitching so that it does not get caught up in the stitching.

Body: Stitch the darts in the 2 back pieces. Pin, baste, and stitch the 2 back pieces together, right sides facing, from point **b** to point **j**.
Stitch the tail pieces together around the curved edge, right sides facing. Turn and stuff. Pin the tail to the right side of the front body where

indicated; stitch it along seamline. Now pin front and back body pieces together, right sides facing, leaving openings at paws and neck. Catch in the tail in stitching. Snip into the seam allowance at the corners and curves. Turn to the right side.

Head: Pin and stitch the upper head pieces together, right sides facing, matching points **c**; stitch the lower head pieces, matching points **d**. Stitch the upper head section to the side pieces, matching points **e**; then stitch the lower head section to the side pieces, matching points **f**.
Now join the snout pieces together, matching all markings. Stitch the snout to the head, matching points **i** and working from each corner to the next separately and finishing the thread off securely every time. Snip diagonally into the seam allowance at the corner of each side head piece. With double buttonhole thread, sew a line of running stitches right around the snout/head seamline. This thread is used later for shaping the head. Stitch the ears together around the curved edge, right sides facing. Turn to the right side and sew the straight edge by hand.

Here is the graph pattern for the pieces to make the cuddly polar bear in the photograph:
1 Body front. **2** Body back. **3** Side of head. **4** Upper head 1. **5** Upper head 2. **6** Lower head 1. **7** Lower head 2. **8** Snout side. **9** Upper snout. **10** Lower snout. **11** Ear. **12** Nose. **13** Back paw. **14** Front paw. **15** Tail.

Sew the ears to the side head at the positions marked.

The head is now ready to stitch to the body. The slit marked on the body front must be cut open to enable the pieces to be pinned together right sides facing. Distribute the ease evenly and stitch. Now pull the head back to the right side.

Cut the fur pile short on the snout and inside the ears. Attach the eyes firmly on the snout seamline. Stuff the head and legs firmly, shaping the snout slightly by pulling up the buttonhole thread.

Sew a few crossed threads loosely across head and leg openings to prevent the stuffing falling back into the body. Now stuff the body loosely so that it retains a soft, floppy shape. After stuffing, sew up the slit firmly by hand.

Finally, sew on the nose and paws, turning under the seam allowance. If using fur fabric, cut the pile short on the nose and paws in the same way as on the snout and ears.

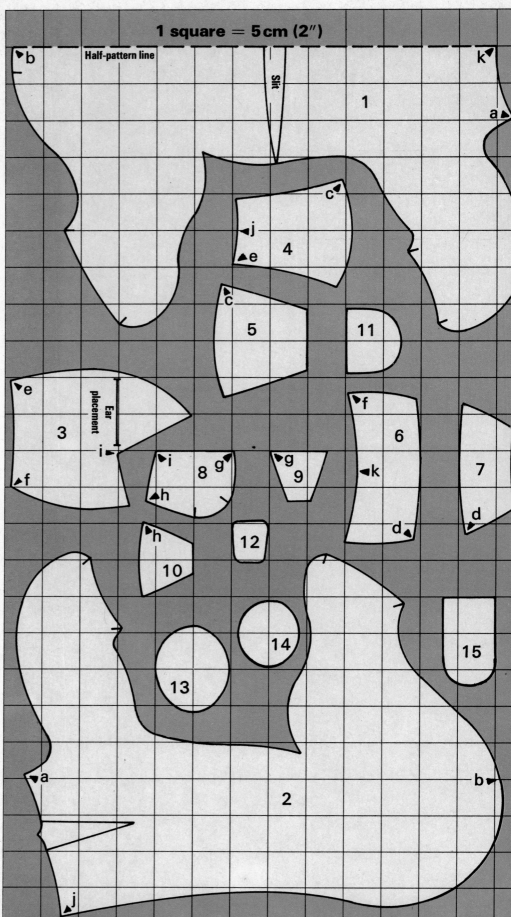

1 square = 5 cm (2″)

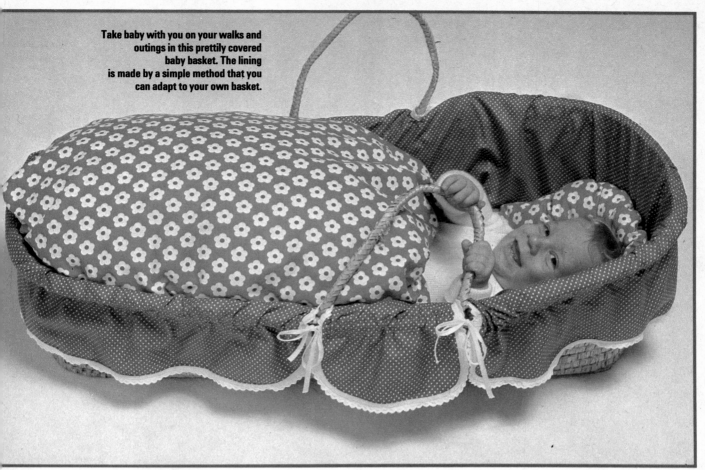

Take baby with you on your walks and outings in this prettily covered baby basket. The lining is made by a simple method that you can adapt to your own basket.

Travelling in style

Size: Our basket measures approximately 80 cm (31½") long by 30 cm (12") wide at the base. The sides rise from 15 cm (6") at foot to 22 cm (8½") at the head.

Lining
Materials Required:
Cotton fabric: 1.65 m (1⅞ yds), 90 cm (36") wide.

White rickrack braid: 3 m (3¼ yds). White bias binding: 4 m (4⅜ yds). White tape: 2 cm (¾") wide, 2.70 m (3 yds). Narrow elastic: 2.20 m (2⅜ yds). Unbleached cotton: 0.65 m (¾ yd), 90 cm (36") wide. Kapok.

Draw around the base shape on a piece of paper. Cut out the fabric with a 1 cm (⅜") seam allowance. Cut out 2 side pieces to fit around the top circumference, adding about 30 cm (12") to the length of each for gathering. Join the side seams and gather in the width at the bottom to fit the base. Stitch the sides and base together. Cut slits for the handles, rounding off the corners. Bind the outer edges and slits with bias binding. Stitch rickrack below it. Stitch the tape onto the wrong side of the lining, just below the fold-over, to make a casing for the elastic. Thread elastic pieces through the head, handle, and foot sections. Draw them up to fit. Sew lengths of bias binding to the

elastic ends to tie as bows around the handles.

Using the base pattern, make a cushion from the unbleached cotton and stuff with kapok.

Pillow and blanket covers
Materials Required:
Cotton. For Both: 1.30 m (1⅜ yds), 90 cm (36") wide.

Blanket cover: Cut 2 pieces to fit the basket, plus 1 cm (⅜") seam allowance. Stitch together around 3 sides. Close 4th side with press studs or snaps. Fold blanket to shape and insert.

Pillow cover: Cut 2 pieces to fit basket, plus 1 cm (⅜") seam allowance. Stitch, turn, fill with kapok or insert a baby pillow.

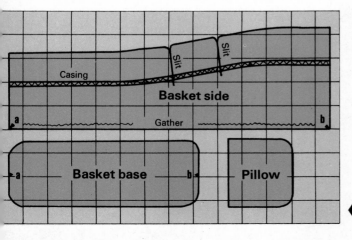

◄ The diagram shows the lining pieces for an average basket. Each square is 10 cm x 10 cm (4" x 4"). Adapt the basic pattern to fit your own basket.

Size: The clothes will fit a toy rabbit approximately 40 cm (15¾") high, excluding ears.

Note: The pattern pieces are on Pattern Sheet 65. Add 0.5 cm (¼") seam allowances unless otherwise indicated.

FEMALES

Cutting out: All pattern pieces are given except the skirts. For these, cut 1 straight strip 66 cm (26") wide and 16 cm (6¼") long, plus seam allowances.

Daughter: Collar: Cut one each in fabric and iron-on interfacing with 0.5 cm (¼") seam allowance at neck only. Iron on the interfacing.

Bow: Cut 2 strips each 9 cm (3½") wide and 16 cm (6¼") long plus allowance and 1 strip 2 cm (¾") wide and 5 cm (2") long plus allowance.

Mother: Apron tie band and waistband (in one): Cut strip 1.5 cm (⅝") wide and 75 cm (29½") long.

Grandma: Front edge and neck of bodice: Cut one bias strip 2 cm (¾") wide and about 34 cm (13½") long. Sash: Cut 1 strip 8 cm (3") wide and 80 cm (31½") long. Bonnet: Cut a circle with a radius of 9 cm (3½").

Sewing: Daughter: Bodice: Join side and shoulder seams. Press under seam allowance at center back. Work blanket stitch around outside of collar. Stitch collar to neck edge, right side to wrong side; turn, and stitch close to edge. Sleeve: stitch hem allowance under. Make pleat by placing points X onto O and fasten with a button. Gather sleeve top, join sleeve seam, and set in sleeve. Skirt: Join the center back seam for 12 cm (4¾") from hem edge. Stitch under hem allowance. Gather waist to bodice measurement and stitch skirt to bodice, right sides facing. Insert 15 cm (6") zipper. Bow: Stitch large strips together and turn. Wrap small strip around longer ones at center, sew together, and fasten to head.

Mother: Bodice: Join side and shoulder seams. Turn seam allowance at neck edge to inside. Press under seam allowance at center back. Neck edge: Cut lace edging 40 cm (15¾") long and gather to neck measurement. Pin this, edge to edge, around neck edge, wrong side to right side, and zigzag-stitch together. Sleeve: Baste lace over the lower tuck line. Pin upper tuck line to lower tuck line, right sides facing, with the lace between. Stitch together from the wrong side. Turn under hem and stitch 2nd lace insertion underneath. Gather sleeve top, join sleeve seam, and insert sleeve. Skirt: See instructions for Daughter. Apron: Stitch on lace insertion with small zigzag stitches and cut away the fabric underneath. Turn under sides and hem. Make pleats by placing points X onto O and stitch. Stitch on waistband with zigzag stitching and finish tie band all around. Shawl: Stitch seams under and trim with fringe border.

Grandma: Bodice: Join shoulder seams. To bind neck and front edges, stitch on bias strip, right sides facing, turn to inside, turn in seam allowance and sew on by hand along the stitching line. Sleeve: Stitch under hem allowance, then stitch on lace edging. Make pleat at sleeve top, join sleeve seam, and insert sleeve. Sew on 2 press studs or snaps at bodice center front. Stitch and turn sash. Skirt: Join center front seam, leaving 6 cm (2½") open at top for slit. Stitch under hem allowance and trim with lace. Gather skirt to bodice width and stitch skirt to bodice, right sides facing. Bonnet: Stitch lace edging around outer edge, wrong side to right side, with small zigzag stitches. On the wrong side, about 1.5 cm (⅝") from the edge, sew on a piece of elastic 27 cm (10½") long. In the center, cut two slits for the ears.

MALES

Cutting out: Shirt: Cut 1 bias strip for neck edge 2 cm (¾") wide and about 21 cm (8¼") long. Seam allowances: At front edge 1.5 cm (⅝"), elsewhere 0.5 cm (¼"). Pants: Cut out 2 front and 2 back parts. Seam allowances: At waist and hem 1.5 cm (⅝"), elsewhere 0.5 cm (¼").

Father: Cut 2 straps each 4 cm (1½") wide and 25 cm (10") long. Cut out 2 felt hearts without seam allowance. Peaked cap: Cut out twice with 0.5 cm (¼") seam allowance all around. Elastic: 1 cm (⅜") wide and 9 cm (3½") long. Scarf: Use a small handkerchief.

Grandpa: Waistcoat: Line with a piece of the shirt fabric.

Sewing: Shirt: Turn under front edges and stitch. Grandpa: Gather neck edge at front. Join side and shoulder seams. Father: Gather neck edge to about 21 cm (8¼"). To bind neck edge, stitch on bias strip, right sides facing. Turn to inside, turn under seam allowance, and sew along stitching line by hand. Stitch under hem allowance and sleeve hem. Father: Trim sleeve with rickrack braid. Gather sleeve top, join sleeve seam, and insert sleeve. Sew press studs or snaps on at front opening. Father: Sew on buttons. Grandpa: Make a bow from braid and sew on. Pants: Father: Stitch hearts to front of pants with zigzag stitching. Join outside leg seams (up to slit sign only on left), then the inside ones. Stitch down seam allowance along slit. Stitch down seam allowance at waist, draw elastic through. Sew on hook and eye at side. Stitch up hem. Father: Stitch and turn straps and sew on at back of pants. Cross over and fasten with buttons at front. Peaked cap: Stitch and turn. Top-stitch all around. Fasten elastic at ends. Grandpa: Waistcoat: Stitch lining to front and back except at sides and shoulders, turn through. Top-stitch edges. Join shoulder and side seams. Sew 2 press studs or snaps to front edges. Sew on buttons.

Rabbit warren

Dress up your toy rabbits with some smart clothes made from bright fabric remnants. The patterns are on Pattern Sheet 65.

Grandpa

Mother

Father

Grandma

Daughter

So easy to make

For young swingers

Here's a hammock specially designed for younger children. It's perfect for those long summer days and rolls up compactly to take on picnics. Made of heavy, unbleached cotton it's tough enough to withstand any amount of swinging, and is very quick and simple to construct.

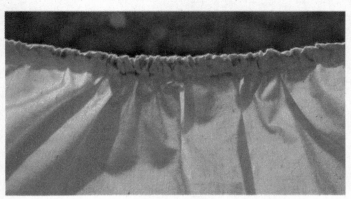

Here you can see one of the long sides of the hammock. A length of cord is drawn through a casing and the fabric is gathered up along it.

The wooden strips at each short side have a notch cut into each end. The rope is fastened so that it rests in the notch and cannot slip out.

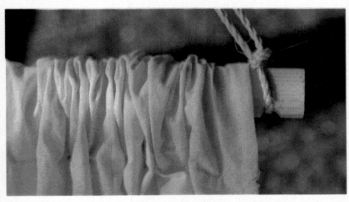

The wooden strip is pushed through a wide casing at each end of the hammock and the fabric is gathered up to expose the notches at either end.

It is very important to fix the rope for hanging securely to a tree or hook. Make a suitably strong knot which cannot slip or work undone.

Materials Required:

Be sure you use strong materials which will stand up to a lot of wear and tear. Heavy unbleached cotton: 3.10 m (3⅜ yds), 90 cm (36″) wide. 2 wooden strips: 60 cm (23¾″) long, 5 cm (2″) wide, and 2 cm (¾″) thick. Thick cord: 1.60 m (1¾ yds). Strong rope, such as a washing line. (Use plenty of rope to enable you to hang the hammock on higher or wider-spaced trees if necessary.)

Making the hammock

Cut the 3.10 m (3½ yds) length of fabric widthwise into 2 pieces [i.e., each piece measures 1.55 m (1¾ yds)]. With right sides facing, stitch the 2 pieces together along both long edges, close to the selvages. Turn to the right side, then make a 1.5 cm (⅝″) hem along each long side, thus forming a casing for the cord. Cut the cord in half and pull through the casing on each side. Gather up the fabric to measure 76 cm (30″) and pin firmly to the cord to hold the ends in place.

On the short sides, make casings for the wooden strips. Turn under raw edges 1 cm (⅜″), then 10 cm (4″). Stitch down twice, catching in the ends of the cord. (If the cord is too thick for the sewing machine, sew it securely by hand).

Make a notch at each end of the wooden strips, 3 cm (1¼″) away from the edge. Push the strips through the 2 wide casings and gather up the fabric until the notches are exposed.

Knot a length of rope into each notch so that it cannot slip out. Then at each end of the hammock, knot the lengths of rope together at a point equidistant from the notches (see large photograph). The hammock is now ready to hang.

For relaxing out-of-doors

Why rough it on your summer picnics and outings this year, when you can relax in comfort on the practical foam mattress which converts easily into a chair?

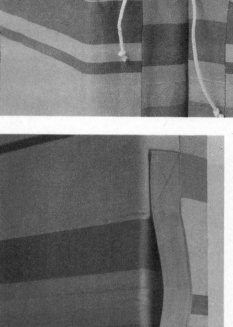

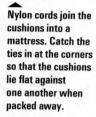

▲ Nylon cords join the cushions into a mattress. Catch the ties in at the corners so that the cushions lie flat against one another when packed away.

◀ Two of the cushions have handles which are stitched on off-center so that they lie close together for carrying purposes.

If you wish to prop up the cushions as a chair, connect the back 2 sections with a strip of fabric and 2 buttons at either side to hold them firm.
▼

Size: 55 cm x 55 cm x 10 cm (21½" x 21½" x 4").

Materials Required: Canvas: 2.10 m (2¼ yds), 140 cm (54") wide *or* 4 m (4⅜ yds), 90 cm (36") wide. Buttonhole thread. 3 foam rubber pads: 55 cm x 55 cm x 10 cm (21½" x 21½" x 4"). Nylon cord: 2.40 m (2⅝ yds). Heavyweight sewing machine needle. 4 buttons.

Cutting out: Cut out each cover, plus 1 cm (⅜") seam allowance all around. For handles and connecting strips: Cut 2 strips for each, measuring 7 cm (2¾") wide by 32 cm (12½") and 45 cm (17¾") long respectively plus seam allowance. Cut 8 cords, each 30 cm (11¾").

Sewing: Join the seams as follows: First stitch along **a–b**, then **c–d**, including the seam allowance at either end. At the remaining open side, stitch 6 cm (2½") at each end. Stitch corners, catching in cords (see photograph). For handles, turn in seam allowance, fold lengthwise, top-stitch all around. Stitch to sides with a decorative cross. Insert cushions; slip-stitch openings. Make connecting strips as for handles, plus buttonholes. Add buttons.

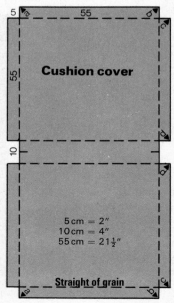

5

55

10

Cushion cover

5 cm = 2"
10 cm = 4"
55 cm = 21½"

Straight of grain

Cut out the cushions according to measurements on the diagram.

Wind screen or play tent

When you're relaxing on the beach, catch the sun and keep out the wind with our versatile canvas wind screen. It doubles as a tent for the children, too. Just add a roof and they can play happily, rain or shine. The construction is very simple — there are four sections and five poles which can be placed in a straight line, a semi-circle or closed into a square as you wish. The roof ties on to the top separately. There's also a zippered ''door'' and useful pockets inside to keep the sand and insects out of your belongings. The screen is held up by guy ropes and tent pegs.

Materials Required:

Canvas: 6.15 m (6¾ yds), 120 cm (48″) wide. Zipper: 60 cm (24″) long (an open-ended one can be used). Dowelling: 5 lengths measuring about 1.40 m (1½ yds). 5 screw eyes, 5 metal eyelets to punch in, 2 metal rings, all 2 cm (¾″) diameter. Strong cord, eg. washing line: about 15 m (16¼ yds). Tent pegs.

Sewing: Cut the 4-section wind screen to measure 120 cm (48″) wide by 4.6 m (5 yds) long plus

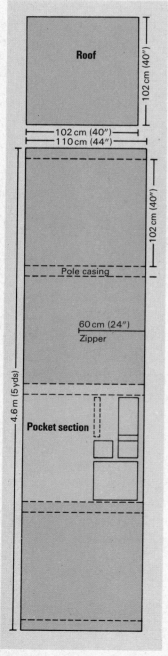

1 cm (⅜″) seam allowance at each short end. Make a 5 cm (2″) hem along both long edges (the height of the wind screen is thus 110 cm (44″). Sew the casings for the dowelling as follows: At the 2 ends, turn in first the seam allowance, then another 10 cm (4″) and stitch down close to the edge. For the 3 inner casings, mark off the 10 cm (4″) divisions as in the diagram. Stitch the fabric together along these lines, thus forming 3 casings for the poles. The width of each section of the wind screen is 102 cm (40″) (see diagram). At the top of each casing, stitch across the fabric to prevent it from slipping down when the poles are inserted. Leave just enough open to fasten a screw eye into each pole.

The guy ropes and the roof are fastened onto the screw eyes with the strong cord. Make sure that the screw eyes are fixed securely into the poles to take the strain.

The poles are sharpened to a point at the lower end, so that they can be pushed into the ground more easily. Before inserting the poles, stitch the various pockets and the zipper into the middle 2 sections of the screen (see the diagram on the right). First stitch

In the diagram on the right, you can see the pocket sizes and how they are positioned on the fabric. Add 1 cm (⅜″) for seams and 5 cm (2″) for the pocket tops.

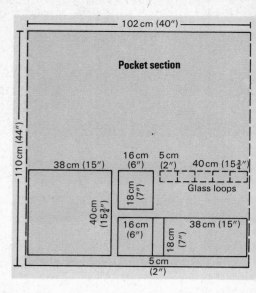

the 5 cm (2″) hems at the pocket top edges. Then press the other seam allowances to the inside and stitch on the pockets. On the long lower pocket, stitch further divisions of 16 cm (6″), 5 cm (2″), and 38 cm (15″).

Make the loops for the glasses to fit your own glasses. Cut the strip for the loops 10 cm (4″) wide plus seam allowance. Stitch together lengthwise and turn, then stitch to the screen at regular intervals. For the zipper, cut a facing strip 63 cm (24¾″) long and 11 cm (4½″) wide plus seam allowances. Press under the seam allowances and stitch the strip over the slit mark around 3 sides. Leave the lower narrow side open. Then cut a 60 cm (24″) slit through both layers of fabric and snip in diagonally 1 cm (⅜″) toward the corners. Turn each edge under 1 cm (⅜″) and baste. Place the zipper in between the layers and stitch in.

Finish the lower edges together with the zipper ends. Punch a metal eyelet to the left and right of the zipper.

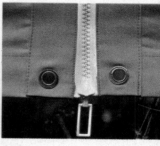

Sew a metal ring to the outside of the fabric at the pole edges on either side of "door" section. The flaps can be fastened with cord to keep the "door" open.

For the tent roof, cut out a 102 cm (40″) square of fabric plus 5 cm (2″) all around for the hem. Stitch the hem, mitering the corners, and then punch an eyelet into each of the corners. The roof can easily be fastened to the tent.

To secure the roof, the 4 corners are fastened to the screw eyes with cord.

Need a quick tote bag?

STYLE 1:
Whether you are going shopping, on a picnic, to the beach, or on a business trip, you always need a handy bag – something that is easy to pack and yet large enough to be really useful. Our tote bag is all of these things, and it's made in easy-to-sew, easy-to-wash sailcloth.

Sewing

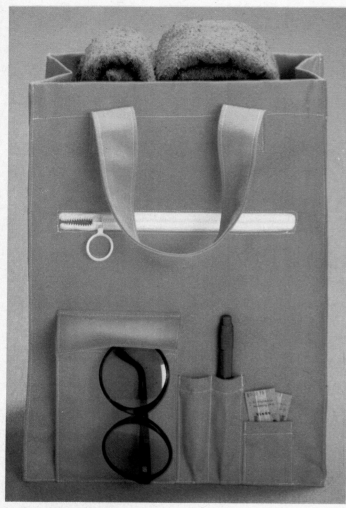

▲ STYLE 2:
STYLE 2:
A bag like this will prove invaluable when you go to the beach or swimming pool, and the bright yellow sailcloth will be cheerful and sunny even if the sun refuses to shine. The side pockets are particularly useful for storing those odd bits and pieces that tend to get lost in the bottom of a bag.

◀ **STYLE 3:**
Sailcloth bags not only look good, but they last for years because the fabric is strong and wears well. The white bag here looks very expensive and is versatile enough to go with every outfit and suit any occasion. Note the smart piping edging the pocket.

Materials Required: Sailcloth for each bag: 1.25 m (1⅜ yd), 100 cm (40") wide. Style 1: White sewing thread. Style 2: 25 cm (10") zipper. White sewing thread. Style 3: Blue bias binding: 55 cm (22") Blue sewing thread.

Drawing the pattern

Draw a pattern on brown paper or tracing paper to the measurements given on the diagram. For Style 1, draw another piece which extends from the bottom edge to line A-B on piece 1. Cut out; pin onto the fabric.

Cutting out

Add seam allowances as follows: add 4 cm (1½") to the upper edge of the front, back, and side pieces, plus the upper edge of the pocket on Style 1. Allow 1 cm (⅜") on all other edges. Cut out the handle twice.

Sewing

Finish all the raw edges except on the handles. Turn under the seam allowance on the upper edges of the front, back, deep pocket on Style 1, and the short edges of the side pieces; turn in all side edges. Stitch 3 cm (1¼") from the top edge of all pieces, catching in the seam allowances of the side seams. Now work the small pockets. In Style 1, these are on the outside of the deep pocket, and on Styles 2 and 3, on the front piece. Fold and stitch along the fold lines of the pleated pocket (pattern piece 4); turn under the seam allowances, and pin in place. Stitch the pocket sides, then form the pleat and stitch the lower edge. To work the pocket flap, turn the seam allowances to the inside, then fold on the fold line, wrong sides facing. Top-stitch the short and folded sides 0.5 cm (³⁄₁₆") from the edge. Top-stitch flap 1 cm (⅜") above pocket.

Stitch under the top edge of the double pocket (pattern piece 6), and then turn under the seam allowance on the other three sides. Pin in position, easing the lower edge into small pleats if necessary, and then stitch the sides, bottom and down the center to form two pockets. Stitch the small pocket (pattern piece 7) along the top edge as for all other pieces, then turn the other sides to the inside. Pin in place and stitch to the bag. For the handles, turn the seam allowances to the inside, fold in half along the fold line and stitch on all sides. Pin in position and top-stitch at points g and h in a decorative cross.

Style 1: The large side pocket extends right across the front, and the seam allowances are turned under and stitched with the side and bottom edges of the front piece.

Style 2: Cut the slit in the front piece and clip diagonally into the corners. Turn under the seam allowances and stitch in the zipper. Fold the pocket lining and stitch the upper and lower edges to the zipper tape; stitch side seams.

Style 3: To work the pocket piping, pin the edges of the bias binding on the right side along each side of the marked line. Stitch on upper and lower seamlines. Cut the slit and clip diagonally into the corners. Turn the binding to the inside; fold pieces so that they meet along line A-B and stitch along the seam. Turn in and sew the corners neatly. Stitch pocket lining to top and bottom of binding.

To assemble bag, turn in remaining seam allowances; pin the side-and-base piece between the front and back pieces, wrong sides together. Top-stitch 0.5 cm (³⁄₁₆") from the side and bottom edges on the front and back pieces

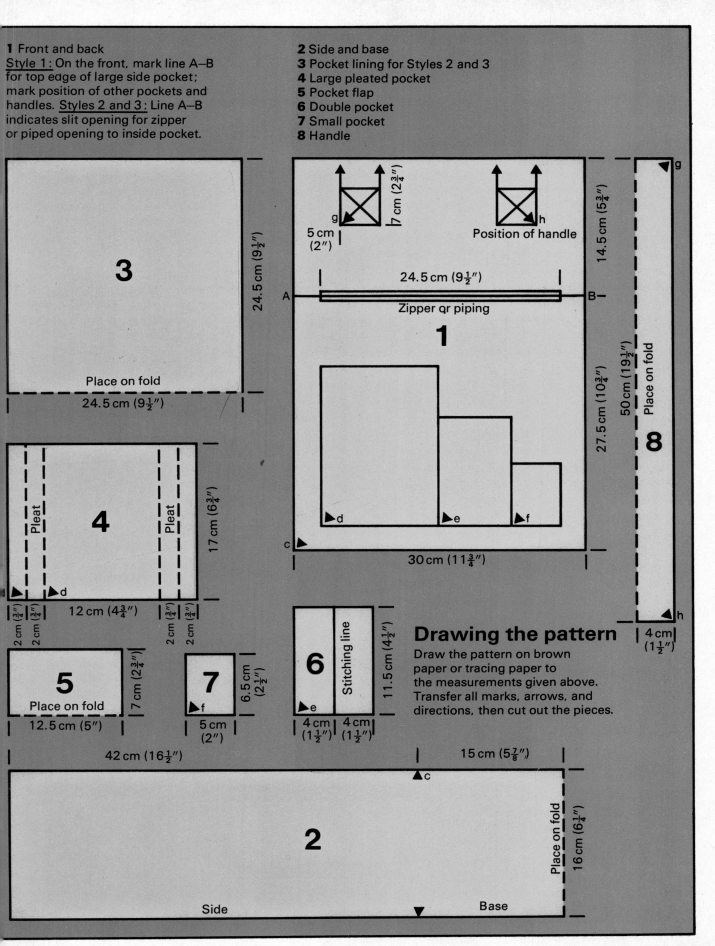

1 Front and back
<u>Style 1</u>: On the front, mark line A–B for top edge of large side pocket; mark position of other pockets and handles. <u>Styles 2 and 3</u>: Line A–B indicates slit opening for zipper or piped opening to inside pocket.

2 Side and base
3 Pocket lining for Styles 2 and 3
4 Large pleated pocket
5 Pocket flap
6 Double pocket
7 Small pocket
8 Handle

3
24.5 cm (9½")
Place on fold
24.5 cm (9½")

5 cm (2")
7 cm (2¾")
g
Position of handle
h
14.5 cm (5¾")

24.5 cm (9½")
A   Zipper or piping   B

1

d   e   f
c
30 cm (11¾")

27.5 cm (10¾")
50 cm (19½")
8
Place on fold
g
h
4 cm (1½")

4
Pleat   Pleat
17 cm (6¾")
d
12 cm (4¾")
2 cm (¾") 2 cm (¾")   2 cm (¾") 2 cm (¾")

5
Place on fold
12.5 cm (5")
7 cm (2¾")

7
f
5 cm (2")
6.5 cm (2½")

6
Stitching line
e
4 cm (1½") 4 cm (1½")
11.5 cm (4½")

Drawing the pattern
Draw the pattern on brown paper or tracing paper to the measurements given above. Transfer all marks, arrows, and directions, then cut out the pieces.

42 cm (16½")
15 cm (5⅞")
c

2
Side   Base
16 cm (6¼")
Place on fold

STYLE 1

Materials Required: Cotton lawn: Size B, 2.70 m (3 yds), 90 cm (36") wide; Size D, 2.75 m (3 yds), 90 cm (36") wide. 4 buttons. Stranded embroidery cotton: 1 skein each in blue, green, yellow, and red.

Cutting out: Pattern pieces are on Pattern Sheet 68. See cutting layout below. Instructions for cutting out are given on Pattern Sheet 68, Style 1. The cross band is not used.

Before embroidering: Work the pleats on the bodice front (see Pattern Sheet 68, Style 1, Fitting).

Embroidering pleats: Embroider in feather stitch through all three layers of fabric, using half the strands of cotton. See Stitch Diagrams 1 and 2. Colors from center front outward are: 1 row yellow, red, blue, green.

Fitting and Sewing: See Pattern Sheet 68, Style 1.

Final embroidery: Embroider the yoke with lines of feather stitch from neck edge to shoulder in reverse color order. Embroider the edge of the collar and cuffs with 1 row of red.

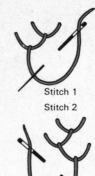

Stitch 1
Stitch 2

STYLE 2

Materials Required: Cotton lawn: Size B: 2.95 m (3¼ yds), 90 cm (36") wide; size D: 3.00 m (3¼ yds), 90 cm (36") wide. 4 buttons. Stranded embroidery cotton: 2 skeins yellow, 1 skein each blue, pale green, green, and red.

Cutting out: Pattern pieces are on Pattern Sheet 68. See cutting layout below. The following pieces are embroidered, so outline them on single fabric with basting, leaving ample room between them: two shoulder yokes, the two cuffs, and the cross band. The fabric with the pattern pieces on it is then cut out from the remainder. Mark the pattern fold lines with basting thread.

Embroidering: Trace the given motif once and once again reverse onto tracing paper. Transfer to the fabric with dressmaker's carbon paper. Place 3 motifs on each shoulder yoke, reversing them as shown in the photograph; place identical motifs on one cuff and reverse them for the other. Place motifs facing each other on the cross band. Work with 2 strands of cotton in stem and satin stitch.

After embroidering: Now cut out the shoulder yokes, cuffs, and cross band, adding 1.5 cm (⅝") seam allowances and then cut out the remaining pattern pieces. Cut the shoulder yoke twice more as it is worked double. Add 2 cm (¾") for hem, elsewhere 1.5 cm (⅝"). For neckband cut a bias strip 4 cm (1½") wide and 40 cm (15¾") long for Size B or 42 cm (16½") long for Size D, plus seam allowance. To bind sleeve slits, cut 2 straight strips 4 cm (1½") wide and 10 cm (4") long. For cuffs, cut 2 pieces of interfacing to the fold line.

Fitting and Sewing: See Pattern Sheet 68, Style 1. Here the seams are not top-stitched and there is a neckband in place of a collar. To make this, press strip in half, stitch short ends, turn. Press into shape by stretching cut edges to 42 cm (16½") for Size B or 44 cm (17⅜") for Size D and easing folded edge to 38 cm (15") for Size B or 40 cm (15¾") for Size D. Stitch single layer of neckband to neck edge, right sides facing, sew inside edge through seam.

Style 1

Above: This fresh-looking blouse in fine lawn is hip length and looks impeccable with pants. The embroidered pleats at the front are released to give the blouse a casual width. The shoulders are embroidered and the collar and cuffs have embroidered edges.

Right: Cutting layouts for the two styles. On this version, small flowers are worked on yoke, cross band, and cuffs. There is a neckband rather than a collar.

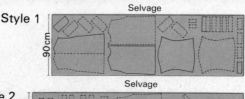

Style 1

Selvage
90 cm
Selvage

Style 2

Selvage
90 cm
Selvage

This is the actual-size pattern for the embroidery motif on Style 2. It is worked in stem and satin stitch in the colors shown.

White's
right for
summer

Style 2

2143

Bulgarian beauty

Here's a re[al]
treat fo[r]
embroiderers [—]
a blouse with [a]
tradition[al]
Bulgarian desig[n.]
It has ragla[n]
sleeves an[d]
a widely-cu[t]
bodice. Th[e]
motifs are [in]
satin stitc[h]
and stem stitc[h]

Size: To fit bust sizes 88 cm–92 cm (34½"–36").

Materials Required: Cotton: 2.10 m (2¼ yds), 90 cm (36") wide. Zipper: 20 cm (8") long. 2 small buttons. Stranded cotton in the following colors and quantities: 3 skeins each yellow, white, and black; 2 skeins each blue and green; 1 skein red. Embroidery frame.

Cutting out: Place the pattern pieces on single fabric as shown on the cutting layout. Mark the outlines and lengthwise fold lines of collar and cuffs with basting. Add 2 cm (¾") for the hem; elsewhere add 1 cm (⅜") seam allowance.

Positioning motifs: The embroidery motifs are given as an actual-size pattern. With dressmaker's carbon paper, transfer the front motif centrally, 7 cm (2¾") away from the neck edge. Transfer the 6 small tulip motifs onto the sleeve 3 cm (1") from the neck edge; transfer the main sleeve motif 1 cm (⅜") below this, then keep adding the small tulip motifs underneath to fill the space. Transfer the 3 upper tulips 1 cm (⅜") below the motif on the front.

On the neckband and cuffs, transfer the border motifs to one lengthwise half only. For the cuffs, use the shorter flower border, for the neckband the longer one, making sure they are positioned centrally. The tips of the yellow heart-shaped flowers point toward the fold line on the neckband and to the cut edge on the cuffs.

Before embroidering: Finish all cut edges with zigzag stitch. So that the lower edge of sleeves, neckband, and cuffs can be stretched onto the frame, mount them onto remnants of fabric.

Embroidering: Fill in all areas with satin stitch and work all lines in stem stitch. Use half the strands of cotton.

After embroidering: Remove the extra pieces of fabric added for stretching into the frame.

Sewing: Join the center back seam up to beginning of zipper. Stitch side and sleeve seams, leaving sleeve open below arrows. Then stitch sleeves to front and back. Gather the neck edge to the length of the neckband and the lower sleeve edge to the cuff length (excluding underlap). Stitch the 2 narrow ends (center back) of the neckband and turn, then stitch one layer of fabric to the neck edge, right sides facing. Press seam toward the neckband, then turn in the seam allowance of the inside neckband and sew down along the seamline by hand. Stitch in the zipper invisibly at the back up to the upper edge of the neckband.

Finish the sleeve slit with a bias strip. Stitch and turn the cuffs and sew on in the same way as the neckband.

Make a looped fastening for the button on the overlap of the cuff. Sew the button into position on the underlap. Turn up and sew the hem.

Inch equivalents:		
	9 cm = 3½"	19 cm = 7½"
1.5 cm = ⅝"	9.5 cm = 3¾"	22 cm = 8⅝"
2 cm = ¾"	10 cm = 3⅞"	23 cm = 9"
4 cm = 1⅝"	11 cm = 4⅜"	24 cm = 9½"
4.5 cm = 1⅞"	12 cm = 4¾"	28 cm = 11"
6 cm = 2⅜"	13 cm = 5⅛"	41 cm = 16⅛"
6.5 cm = 2⅝"	14 cm = 5½"	42.5 cm = 16¾"
7.5 cm = 3"	16 cm = 6¼"	52 cm = 20½"
8.5 cm = 3⅜"	18.5 cm = 7¼"	61 cm = 24"

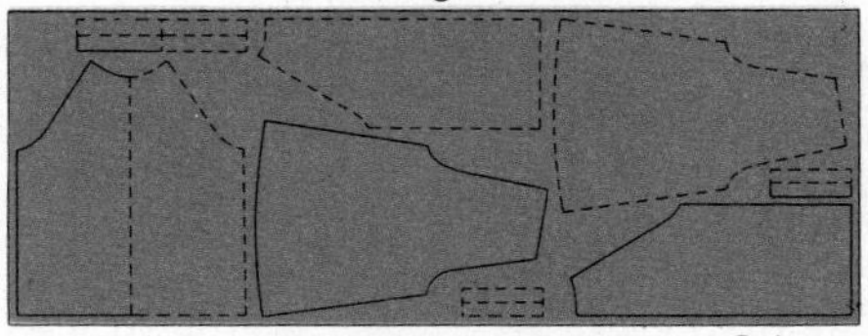

Cutting layout: Place pattern pieces on single fabric as shown above.

The pattern pieces for the blouse are shown below. Draw the pieces to the measurements on the diagram. The numbers are centimeters; inch equivalents are also given.

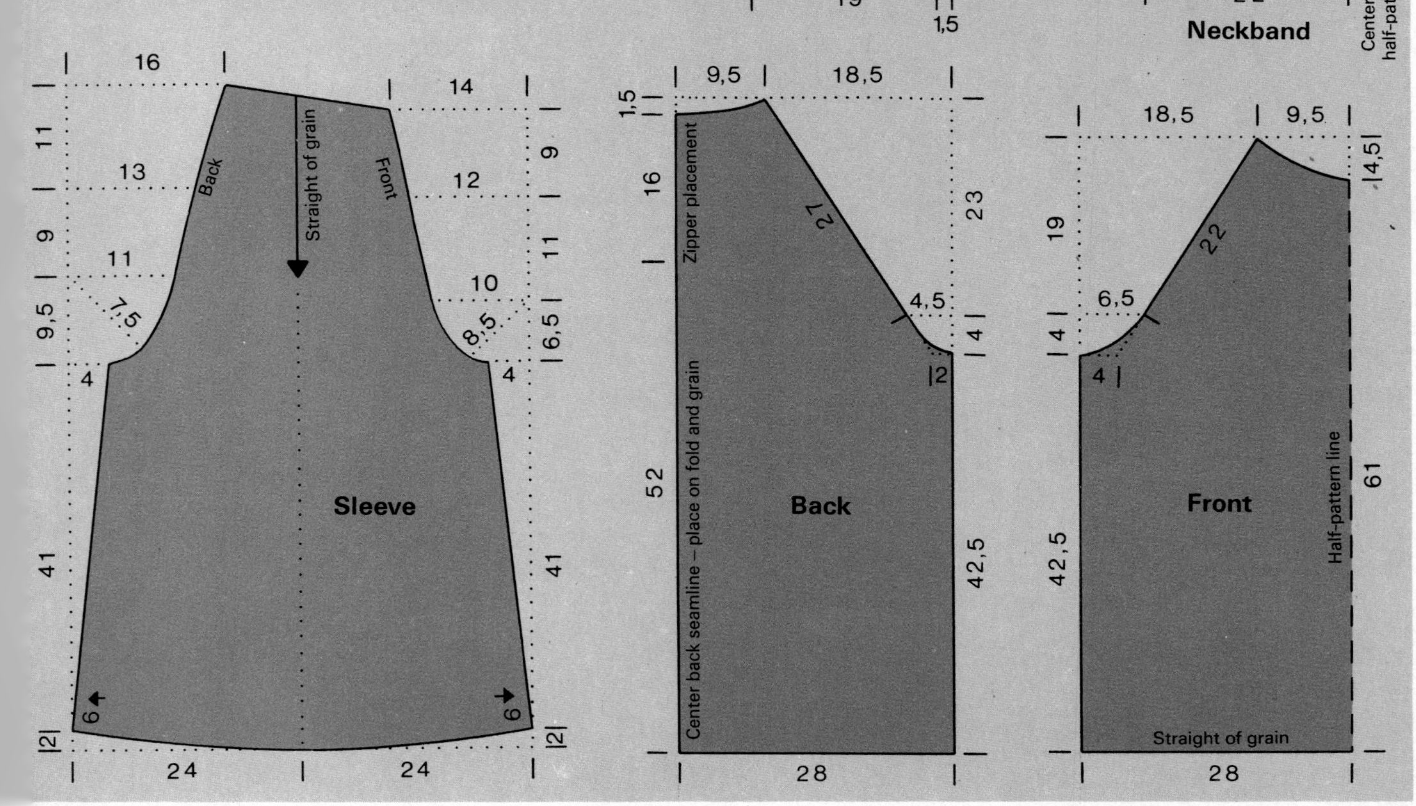

Sleeve

Embroidery for peasant blouse

This stunning embroidery is worked on the collar, cuffs, and bodice of a loose blouse.

A
Neckband – join at points A

Cuff

A

Bodice front

Small tulip motifs

2147

Enter the dragon

Feel luxurious in a silk tunic, embroidered with a traditional Chinese dragon and characters.

Size: To fit 92 cm–96 cm (36″–37½″) bust.

Materials Required:
Silk fabric: 2.30 m (2½ yds), 90 cm (36″) wide. Soft woven interfacing: 0.30 m (⅜ yd), 90 cm (36″) wide. 6 button forms to be covered. Stranded cotton: 3 skeins blue; 2 skeins rust; 1 skein each rose, pale blue, yellow, ochre.

Cutting out: The button-hole band at the raglan sleeve is joined to the front bodice on the diagram. Cut it off before cutting out the fabric. The front bodice and sleeve bands are embroidered before sewing. Roughly cut out these parts only in single fabric. See seam allowances under Final cutting out. Mark the seam outlines with basting.

Embroidering: From the actual-size pattern, transfer the dragon motif to the center of the front with dressmaker's carbon paper, about 4 cm (1½″) from the neck edge, then transfer the sleeve motifs onto the bands. Embroider fine silk fabrics with divided stranded cotton, thicker silks with undivided cotton. Work all large areas with diagonal or long-and-short satin stitch. Use chain stitch for outlining the flames and stem stitch for the dragon's mane. The sleeve motifs are worked in diagonal satin stitch.

Final cutting out: Recut the embroidered pieces to the correct size plus seam allowance. Cut out the remaining parts.

Seam allowance: Add 2 cm (¾″) at front raglan part of sleeve only for the underlap, plus 2 cm (¾″) for seam. Cut out the bands on the front twice on the fold. Cut out front and back collars twice on the fold. Add 3 cm (1¼″) for hem, 2 cm (¾″) for sleeve seams and side seams up to point **b**. Elsewhere, add 1 cm (⅜″).

Cut 2 strips for tie belt 80 cm (31½″) long and 8 cm (3″) wide plus 1 cm (⅜″) all around.

Sewing: Interface the front bands, collar, and underlaps of the raglan sleeves. Fold in the seam allowance of the raglan underlaps and then stitch. Press the front bands in half lengthwise. Stitch the bands to the sleeves, right sides facing and stitching along the band fold line from the underarm to the arrow [11 cm (4⅜″)]. Fold the band along the fold line and stitch to the front through all thicknesses, right sides facing. Finish

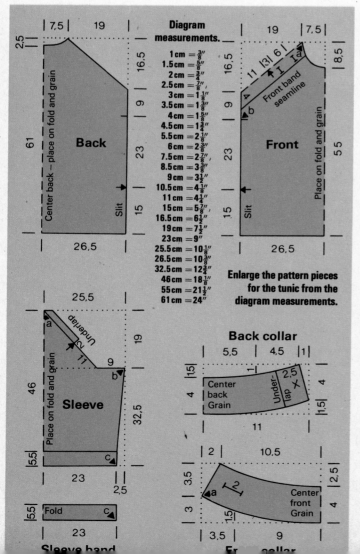

Diagram measurements.

1 cm	= ⅜″
1.5 cm	= ⅝″
2 cm	= ¾″
2.5 cm	= ⅞″
3 cm	= 1⅛″
3.5 cm	= 1⅜″
4 cm	= 1⅝″
4.5 cm	= 1¾″
5.5 cm	= 2⅛″
6 cm	= 2⅜″
7.5 cm	= 2⅞″
8.5 cm	= 3⅜″
9 cm	= 3½″
10.5 cm	= 4⅛″
11 cm	= 4¼″
15 cm	= 5⅞″
16.5 cm	= 6½″
19 cm	= 7½″
23 cm	= 9″
25.5 cm	= 10⅛″
26.5 cm	= 10⅜″
32.5 cm	= 12¾″
46 cm	= 18⅛″
55 cm	= 21½″
61 cm	= 24″

Enlarge the pattern pieces for the tunic from the diagram measurements.

w edges. Snip into the am allowance at the derarm corner. Stitch the eeve to the front from the rner to point **b**. Finish am allowances and press en. Join back and sleeve glan seam, snip into the am allowance at the derarm corner, then tch sleeve and back derarm up to point **b**. tch side seams down to row. Join the sleeve ands to a circle and stitch , right side to wrong de of sleeve. Fold the ands to the right side, rn in the seam allow- ces, and stitch to the eeve close to the turned- edge. Stitch the front d back collar pieces gether, leaving the lower dges open. Turn. tch to the front and ack, right sides facing, rough one layer only. The

underlap on the back collar extends beyond the neck edge at each side. Turn in remaining seam allow- ances and sew by hand. Work 2 buttonholes 2 cm ($\frac{3}{4}$″) long into each front band, 1.5 cm ($\frac{5}{8}$″) from the outer edge. Work 1 button- hole 2 cm ($\frac{3}{4}$″) long into the front collar on each side, also 1.5 cm ($\frac{5}{8}$″) from the outer edge. Make covered buttons as follows: cut a circle of fabric double the size of the button. Gather the edge with small stitches. Place the fabric over upper part of button, draw up the thread and fasten off. Press the lower part in place.
Stitch the tie belt strips into 1 long strip. Fold in half lengthwise, right sides facing, and stitch along long sides and 1 short side. Turn to right side and sew last side. Sew hem.

Our Chinese tunic has elbow-length wide raglan sleeves and is buttoned at the shoulder and at the mandarin collar. It has slits at the sides and a tie belt.

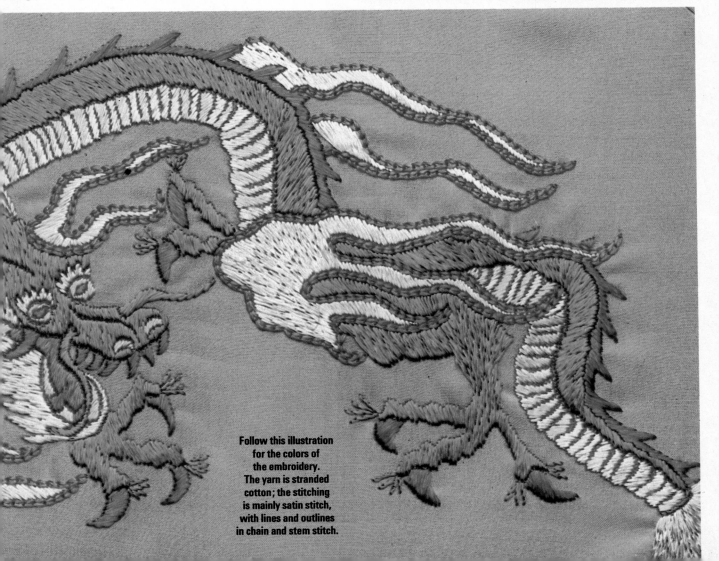

Follow this illustration for the colors of the embroidery. The yarn is stranded cotton; the stitching is mainly satin stitch, with lines and outlines in chain and stem stitch.

Center motif

Half of sleeve motif

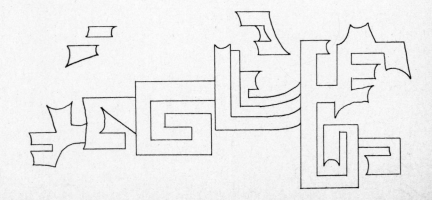

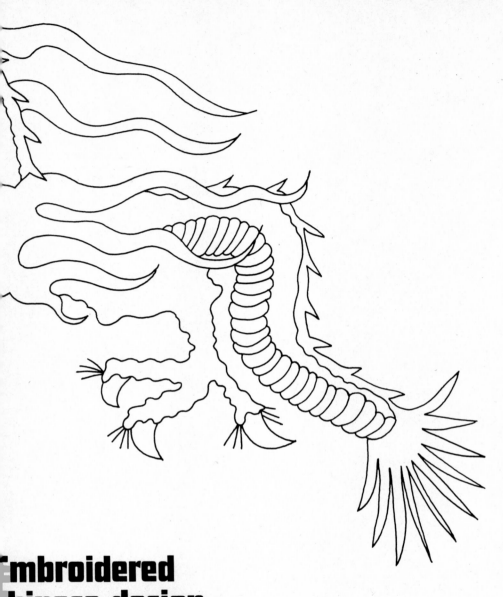

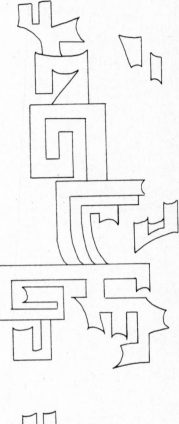

Half of sleeve motif

Embroidered Chinese design

This splendid dragon adorns the front of a silk blouse. Work it in neatly interlocking areas of satin stitch. Embroidered Chinese characters add a further oriental flavor.

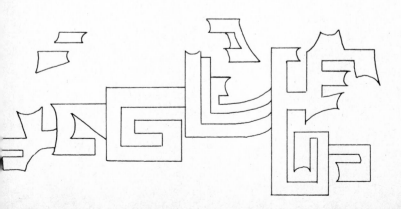

Size: To fit 84 cm–88 cm (33″–34$\frac{1}{2}$″) bust.

Materials Required: Bleached cotton: 1.40 m (1$\frac{1}{2}$ yds), 180 cm (72″) wide. Soft double-thread cross-stitch canvas, 20 holes to 5 cm (10 holes to 1″): 0.40 m ($\frac{1}{2}$ yd), 90 cm (36″) wide. Stranded embroidery cotton: 1 skein each of red, blue, green, yellow, and black. 4 small buttons.

Before cutting out: As the cotton may shrink, wash and iron it before cutting out.

Cutting out: See cutting layout. Enlarge pattern pieces from diagram. Front and back yoke and cuffs are embroidered. Place these pieces onto single fabric, cut front yoke and cuff twice, the back yoke once, adding 1 cm ($\frac{3}{8}$″) seam allowance all around. Cut off the rest of the fabric beyond these pieces. Mark the pattern outlines and fold lines with basting thread and cut out roughly.

Cut out the soft canvas to fit the embroidered parts of the yoke and cuffs. For front yoke, cut separate pieces for horizontal and vertical lines of embroidery. Baste into place on appropriate pattern piece.

Embroidering: Work over the canvas in cross-stitch with 2 strands of cotton, following design from chart. Part of the back yoke motif is also used for cuffs; work left corner with center motif onto right cuff and vice versa. On front yoke, work horizontal section of design first, then remove the canvas thread by thread. After this, work the vertical part; the 2 sections will not join at right angles as the yoke slopes outward toward the shoulder.

After embroidering: Draw out the canvas threads from the embroidered sections one by one. Cut out front and back yokes and cuffs exactly. With the remaining fabric doubled, cut out the rest of the pieces as on cutting layout, adding 1 cm ($\frac{3}{8}$″) seam allowance and 2 cm ($\frac{3}{4}$″) for hem. For sleeve slits, cut 2 straight strips 4 cm (1$\frac{1}{2}$″) wide and 10 cm (4″) long.

Sewing: Join short center seam [1 cm ($\frac{3}{8}$″)] of front yoke. Press under facing along fold line. Gather front and back from center to * to width of relevant yoke, then stitch on. Finish cut edges together. Join side and shoulder seams. Work neckband as follows: stitch upper edge and short sides; turn. Stitch one layer of neckband to neck edge, right sides facing. Turn in the other seam allowance and sew on along seamline. Face sleeve slit with cut strip. Join sleeve seam. Gather sleeve top between * to 18.5 cm (7$\frac{3}{8}$″). Set in sleeves. Gather lower end of sleeve to length of cuff (less underlap). Stitch and turn cuff and stitch on with underlap. Press hem under and stitch. Finally, make 2 loops on each cuff in buttonhole stitch and sew buttons in place on the underlap.

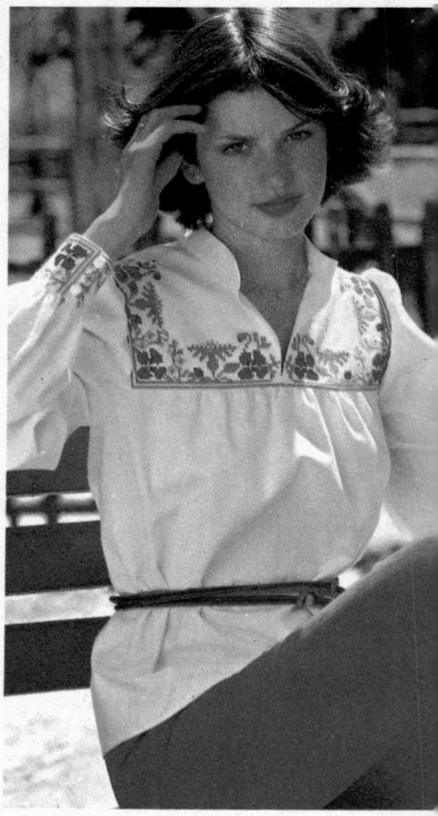

Inch equivalents:

	7.5 cm = 3″	15.5 cm = 6$\frac{1}{8}$
	8 cm = 3$\frac{1}{8}$″	16.5 cm = 6$\frac{5}{8}$
1.5 cm = $\frac{5}{8}$″	8.5 cm = 3$\frac{3}{8}$″	17 cm = 6$\frac{5}{8}$
2 cm = $\frac{3}{4}$″	9 cm = 3$\frac{1}{2}$″	17.5 cm = 7″
2.5 cm = 1″	9.5 cm = 3$\frac{3}{4}$″	18.5 cm = 7$\frac{3}{8}$
3 cm = 1$\frac{1}{8}$″	10 cm = 3$\frac{7}{8}$″	19 cm = 7$\frac{1}{2}$
3.5 cm = 1$\frac{3}{8}$″	10.5 cm = 4$\frac{1}{8}$″	21 cm = 8$\frac{1}{4}$
4 cm = 1$\frac{5}{8}$″	11 cm = 4$\frac{3}{8}$″	26.5 cm = 10
4.5 cm = 1$\frac{7}{8}$″	12 cm = 4$\frac{3}{4}$″	27 cm = 10
5 cm = 2″	12.5 cm = 4$\frac{7}{8}$″	28 cm = 11
5.5 cm = 2$\frac{1}{4}$″	13 cm = 5$\frac{1}{8}$″	38 cm = 15
6 cm = 2$\frac{3}{8}$″	13.5 cm = 5$\frac{3}{8}$″	39 cm = 15
6.5 cm = 2$\frac{5}{8}$″	14 cm = 5$\frac{1}{2}$″	43.5 cm = 17
7 cm = 2$\frac{3}{4}$″	15 cm = 5$\frac{7}{8}$″	46 cm = 18

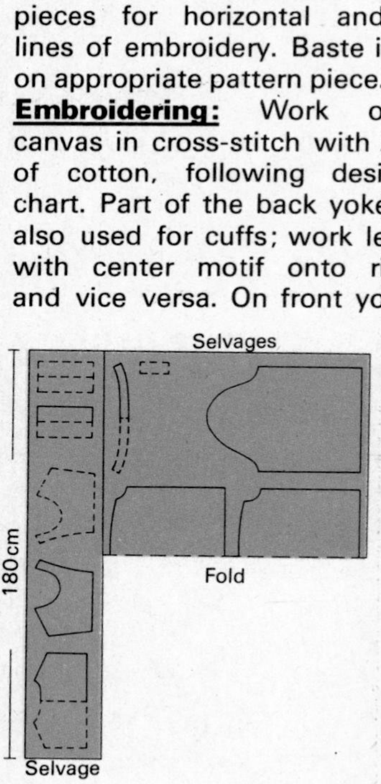

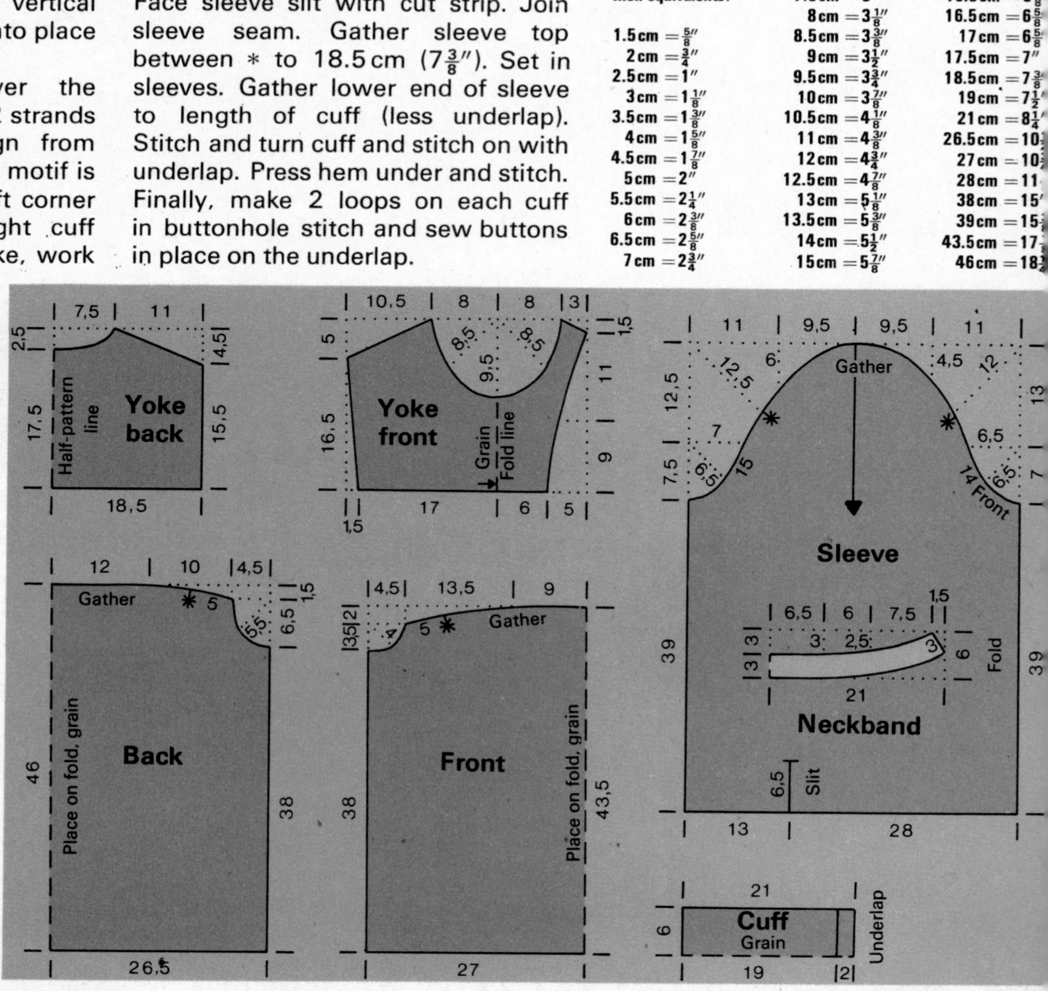

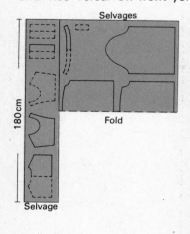

Floral display

Greet the first days of summer in a fresh white embroidered blouse with a flower border worked in cross-stitch.

Horizontal band, right front yoke

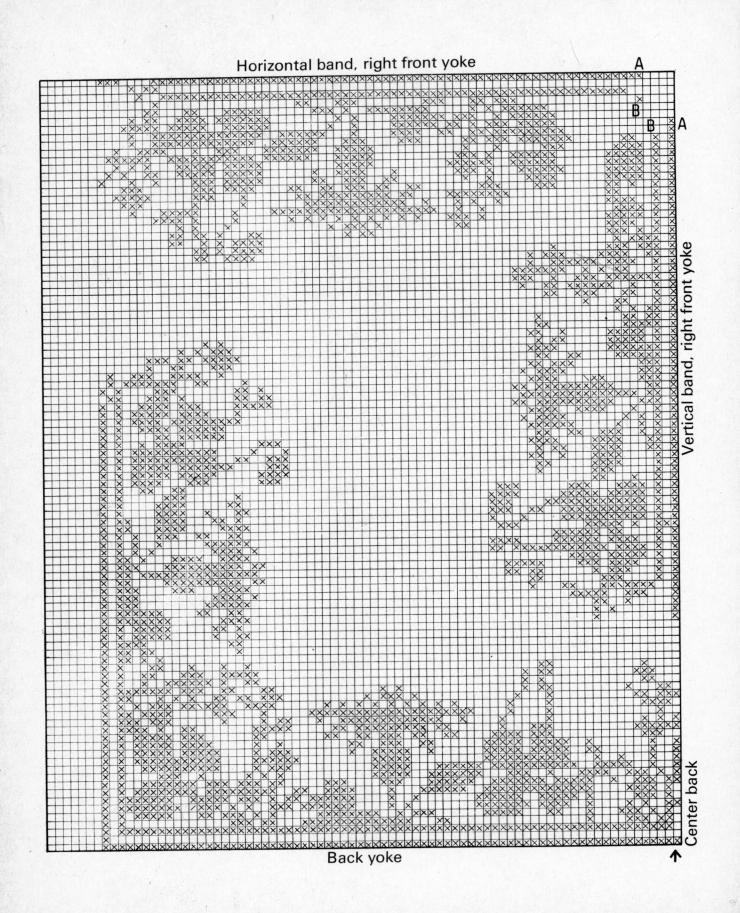

A

B

B A

Vertical band, right front yoke

Center back

Back yoke

Worked in satin stitch
Try a new angle

Size: About 32 cm (12¾") square.
Materials Required: Single-thread canvas: 45 cm (18") square, 14 holes to 2.5 cm (1"). Tapestry yarn: Style 1: 23 m (25 yds) yellow, 46 m (50 yds) lt. green, 39 m (42 yds) each gold and lt. brown, 36 m (39 yds) each dk. green and dk. brown, 10 m (10 yds) orange. Style 2: 62 m (67 yds) dk. pink, 59 m (64 yds) dk. green, 45 m (49 yds) rose, 37 m (40 yds) leaf green, 13 m (14 yds) each salmon pink and lime. Backing fabric 35 cm (14") square. Cushion to fit. Zipper.

Working embroidery and making cover
The cushions are embroidered in straight satin stitches. Follow the relevant chart and work over the number of threads shown. Where 2 colors meet, the yarns emerge from the same hole so that no canvas threads show. Begin each design at the center of the canvas.
For Style 1, one quarter of the design is given; repeat the other quarters as mirror images. For Style 2, one repeat pattern is given. Repeat horizontally and vertically.
Trim canvas edges to 1.5 cm (⅝"). Stitch backing to canvas, right sides facing, on 3 sides. Turn. Sew in zipper on 4th side. Insert cushion.

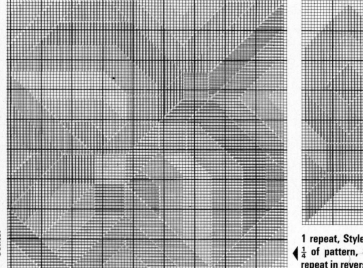

1 repeat, Style 2.
¼ of pattern, Style 1, repeat in reverse.

Style 1

Style 2

Soft selection

These pure white cushion covers show the versatility of satin stitch canvaswork. Take your pick from four fascinating patterns.

Size: Approximately 40 cm x 40 cm (15¾" x 15¾").

Materials Required: Embroidery canvas [28 holes to 5 cm (14 holes to 1")]: for each cushion, 1 piece measuring 52 cm (20½") square. White tapestry yarn: 13 skeins each for Cushions 1 and 4, 10 skeins for Cushion 2, and 9 skeins for Cushion 3; plus 2 skeins per cushion for cord. Backing fabric.

Basic Stitch: Satin stitch.

Working the designs

Leave a border of about 6 cm (2⅜") of unworked canvas all around design area. When working repeats, read chart from left to right and bottom to top respectively. Work the main center pattern first, following appropriate chart. Then add narrow border.

Cushion 1: Work repeat pattern 8 times in width, adding the border strips at beginning and end (205 holes in width). Repeat pattern upward (205 holes).

Cushion 2: Work repeat pattern 8 times in width, adding ½ repeat pattern at end (205 holes in width). Repeat pattern upward (205 holes). Add border strips.

Cushion 3: Begin with the zigzag, *work ½ the vertical repeat pattern upward, adding the center stitch and finish the pattern in reverse. Repeat from * another 7 times upward (216 holes). Continue working zigzags across the canvas in the same way until the design is 216 holes square. Add border strips.

Cushion 4: Work repeat pattern 5 times in width, then add the 6th pattern until work measures 210 holes. Work upward repeat pattern 8½ times (204 holes). Add border strips.

Finishing: Trim the excess canvas down to 3 cm (1¼"). Stitch to the backing fabric on 3 sides and turn. Place cushion inside and sew up. Twist together 8 strands of yarn to make a cord the length of the cushion circumference and sew on all around.

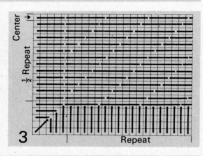

1

2

Counted-thread patterns: Each chart shows 1 repeat pattern in width and part of the upward pattern, plus corner and border strip patterns. The fine lines of the grid represent the weave of the canvas.

3

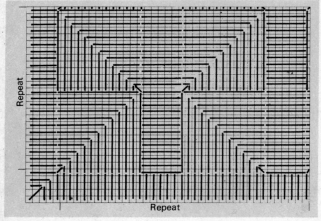

4

2

Showboat Special

This cheerful wall panel depicts a river scene full of activity with people, animals, and boats passing by.

Size: Approximately 69.5 cm x 139 cm ($27\frac{1}{2}$" x $54\frac{3}{4}$").

Materials Required: Skeined rug wool (25 gm or 1 oz skeins): 1 skein each of orange, burgundy, scarlet, cornflower blue, dark blue, violet, pale violet, rose, aubergine, black, pale turquoise, brown, dark brown, yellow, turquoise, pale yellow, white; 2 skeins each of bottle green, olive, pale olive, gold, pale blue; 3 skeins each of blue and lime. Double-thread canvas: 14 holes to 5 cm (7 holes to 1"), 1.60 m ($1\frac{3}{4}$ yds), 90 cm (36") wide. Large tapestry needle. 2 narrow wooden battens: about 139 cm ($54\frac{3}{4}$") long for hanging.

Basic Stitch: Vertical Florentine or Bargello stitch.

Working the piece

The vertical Florentine or Bargello stitch is worked here over 3 horizontal threads of canvas. The needle is taken diagonally across at the back to begin the next stitch.

Mark the center of the piece of canvas and begin stitching here, following the colors indicated on the chart, overleaf. Each square on the chart represents 3 adjacent stitches in the appropriate color worked over 3 horizontal threads. Fill in the larger areas of color first, then go back and fill in the smaller areas later.

When the piece is complete, trim the excess canvas to about 5 cm (2"). Fold back and stitch down, leaving the ends open at top and bottom so that the wooden battens can be drawn through for hanging.

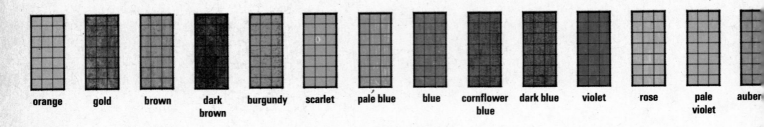
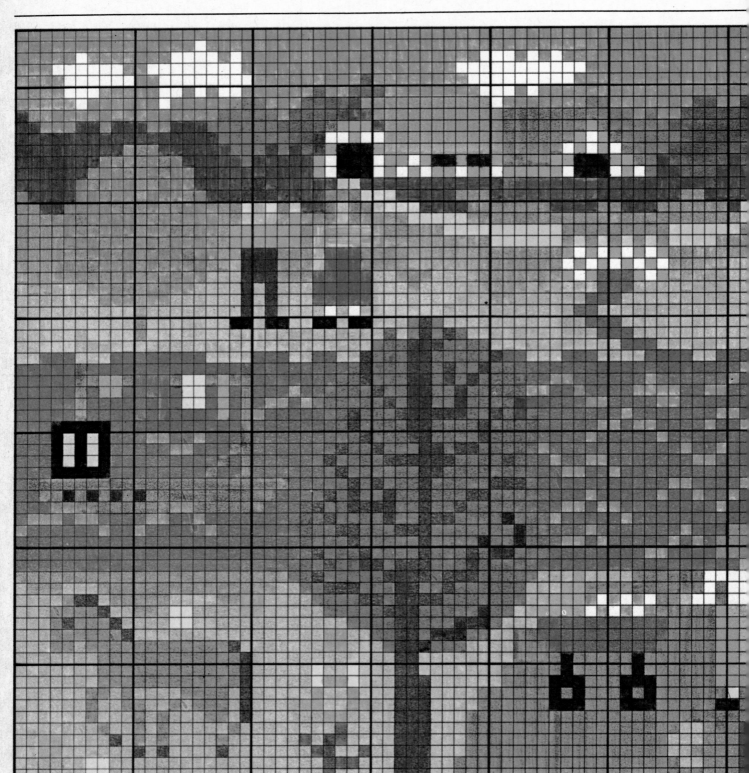

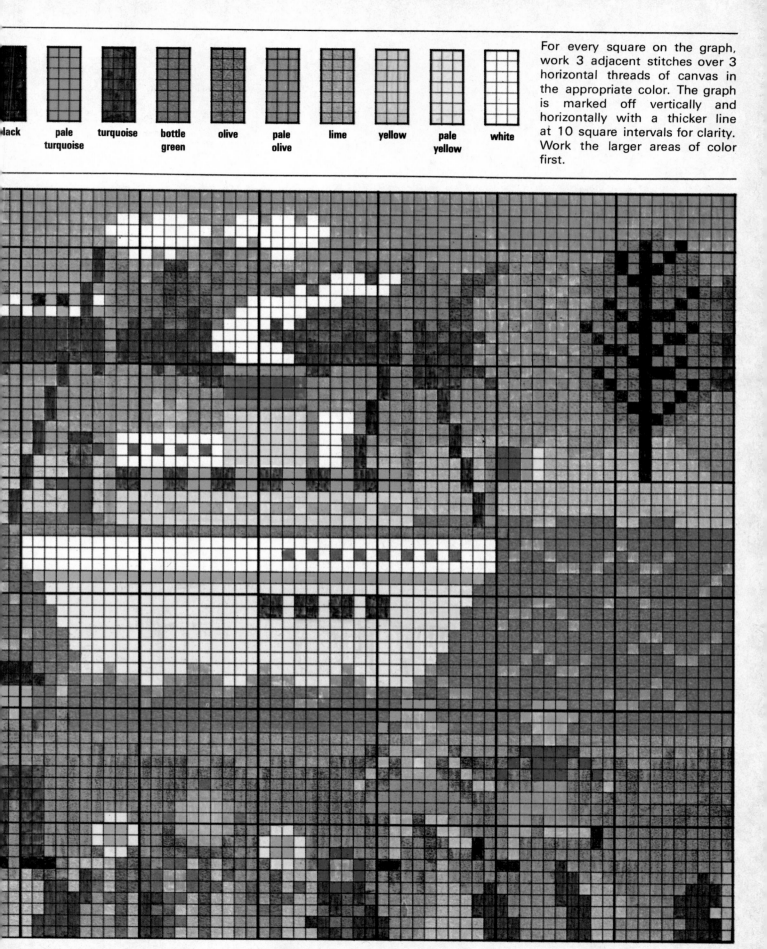

black pale turquoise turquoise bottle green olive pale olive lime yellow pale yellow white

For every square on the graph, work 3 adjacent stitches over 3 horizontal threads of canvas in the appropriate color. The graph is marked off vertically and horizontally with a thicker line at 10 square intervals for clarity. Work the larger areas of color first.

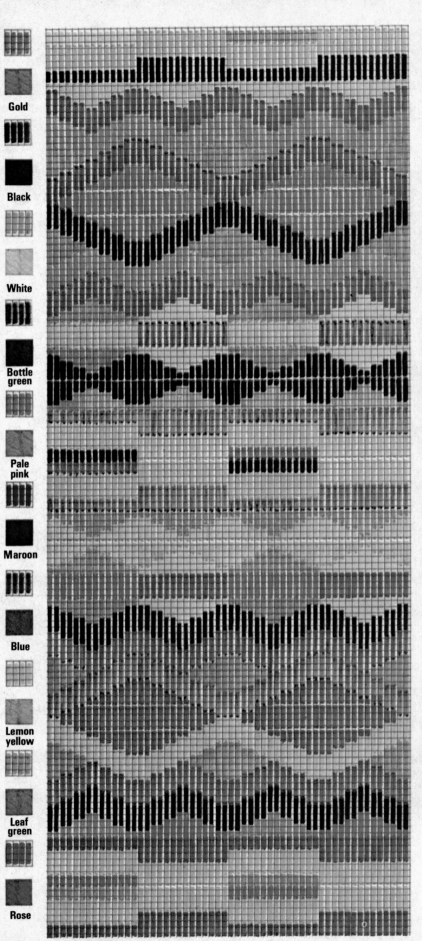

Gold

Black

White

Bottle
green

Pale
pink

Maroon

Blue

Lemon
yellow

Leaf
green

Rose

Mexican
magic

If you would like a
larger rug, either add
more repeat patterns
widthways and lengthways
or work on a larger-mesh
canvas with thicker wool.
You may need to join
strips of canvas for
sufficient width.

Size: Approximately 148 cm x 75 cm (58½" x 30").

Materials Required: Double-thread rug canvas, 10 holes to 5 cm (2"): 1.60 m (1¾ yds), 90 cm (36") wide. Carpet tape: 4.60 m (5 yds). Several rug needles with rounded ends. Rug wool [25 gm = 25 m or 27 yds]: 175 gm or 7 oz each black, white, maroon; 125 gm or 5 oz each gold, bottle green, pale pink, blue, leaf green; 100 gm or 4 oz rose; 50 gm or 2 oz lemon yellow.

Working the rug

Leave 5 cm (2") border of unworked canvas all around. Work rug as shown overleaf, following chart and color key opposite. The chart shows one section of the pattern; repeat this 5½ times in width. When one half of rug is finished, complete other half as mirror image. To finish, turn back unworked canvas; cover raw edge with tape.

Satin stitch on canvas

1 Bring the thread through one of the larger holes, take it over 4 horizontal pairs of threads and insert again into the larger hole directly above. Bring the needle out again at the next smaller hole along at bottom, ready to begin the next stitch.

2 Work the second stitch like the first one, but here the thread emerges from the small hole, it is inserted into the small hole above it, and brought out at the next larger hole at bottom. Leave 4 horizontal pairs of threads between.

3 Work one stitch next to the other in this way, always inserting the needle into alternately large holes and small ones. The stitches lie parallel to one another vertically. On the reverse side, the stitches are slightly slanting.

4 The next row is simply worked above the previous one and both rows share the same holes where they meet. Here a green row is worked above a red row.

5 If the design shows a color which spans more than 5 holes, work two rows of the same color so that the threads butt up against each other.

6 By varying the number of holes over which stitches are worked, rectangular, diamond, and zigzag shapes are created. The next row fills in the spaces.

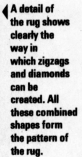

◄ A detail of the rug shows clearly the way in which zigzags and diamonds can be created. All these combined shapes form the pattern of the rug.

Another ► section shows rectangles of different colors set in a staggered pattern. There are also rows of triangles and diamonds.

Colors and quantities are shown in the key on the left. Each skein is 25 m or 28 yds. ¼ of the design is given.

Size: Approximately 127 cm x 158 cm (50" x 63½").

Materials Required:
Double-thread rug canvas, 20 threads to 4 cm (5 threads to 1"): 4 m (4⅜ yds), 90 cm (36") wide. Skeined rug wool in the colors and quantities shown overleaf. Large-size tapestry needles. Carpet tape.

Making the rug
Cut the canvas crosswise into 2 panels of 2 m (2³⁄₁₆ yds). Cut 1 selvage off each panel and place these edges of the panels side by side, overlapping about 4 or 5 squares exactly with those beneath. Sew together with long stitches. Begin the embroidery at least 5–6 cm (2"–2⅜") from the edges. Thread a separate needle with each color to avoid continually changing as you work. Following the chart overleaf, work the stitches as shown, always moving from left to right, then right to left. Draw the beginning and end of the wool under the stitches on the wrong side. Quarter of the design is shown. Work the other 3 quarters as mirror images. Complete each area of one color before moving on to the next; this is simpler than working in rows right across the canvas. When you reach the overlapping canvas in the center, simply work the stitches through the double canvas.

When the pattern is complete, the rug will need to be blocked because the diagonal slant of the stitches will pull the canvas out of shape. Block the rug on a large board covered with brown paper. Draw the outline of the rug on the paper and fasten on the rug with rustproof thumbtacks or drawing pins. Dampen slightly and leave to dry completely. After blocking, fold the raw edges to the inside and sew carpet tape over them all around.

1 Here are some of the colors of the rug wool you will need for the embroidery. It is chunky and easy to use, and also hard-wearing. In all, we used 13 colors.

2 To work the 1st row of the stitch, bring the needle out from the bottom, then insert it diagonally upward one hole along to the right. Bring it out again in the hole immediately below. Continue to the end of the color area.

3 After the last stitch of the previous row, take the needle horizontally 1 hole to the left, then diagonally upward to the right. Bring it out again through the next free hole on the left. Row 3: Repeat photograph 2. Row 4: Repeat photograph 3.

4 Embroider the canvas, section by section, leaving spaces for the stitches of other colors to be filled in. This avoids changing color frequently.

5 The stitches lie on the canvas like rows of little beads. This technique is particularly suitable for quite complex designs where the detail must show clearly.

Country life

A wall hanging or
rug to work in
tent stitch with
a folk motif border.

Jumbo rug

Elephants parade trunk to tail around this magnificent rug. The neutral colors and geometric central pattern blend well with many styles of furniture and decor.

Size: Approximately 160 cm x 205 cm (63" x 82").

Materials Required: Rug canvas, $3\frac{1}{3}$ holes to 2.5 cm (1"): 4.40 m ($4\frac{7}{8}$ yds), 90 cm (36") wide. Pre-cut rug wool in packs of 320 strands: 69 packs black; 45 packs beige; 71 packs white. Carpet tape: 7.50 m ($8\frac{1}{4}$ yds). Buttonhole thread.

Making the rug

Cut canvas in half width-wise. The rug can either be worked straight across its width by joining the canvas before hooking, or, if you find this too large to handle, it can be worked in 2 equal sections and joined afterward. In this case, make sure the pile on each section runs in the same direction.

To work the rug in one piece, cut 1 lengthwise selvage from each canvas strip and join strips by overlapping these edges by 5 cm (2"), matching up holes exactly. Sew together with diagonal basting stitches.

Work rug from chart, overleaf, which shows $\frac{1}{4}$ of design. Each square represents 1 knot. Leave a border of at least 5 cm (2") all around. Using the Smyrna knot described right, hook in rows from left to right (or vice versa if left-handed.)

When the rug is complete, trim the excess canvas to 5 cm (2") all around, turn it back and stitch down with buttonhole thread. Cover raw ends with carpet tape, sewn on by hand.

Either of the types of canvas above can be used. Ordinary double-weave canvas is on the left, a twisted warp on the right.

1 To work the Smyrna knot, pass the hook under 2 cross threads from bottom to top, place a strand of rug wool in the hook and draw it through.

2 Turn the strand ends to the left. Push the hook up through the loop of wool so that the latch passes through and opens.

3 Lay the ends of the strand across the hooked end from left to right (or vice versa if you prefer) and pull the hook downward. The latch will close and draw the ends of the strand through the loop. Pull the ends firmly to an even length to secure.

4 The finished Smyrna knot is shown above. The ends of all the strands build up the thick pile of the rug, which will be very hard-wearing.

The chart shows $\frac{1}{4}$ of the design. Each square represents 1 knot. Begin knotting at lower left-hand corner and follow chart across to right-hand corner. Continue across the canvas, reading the chart in reverse and omitting the center square. Continue up the chart row by row in this way until the lower half of the rug is complete. For the upper half, repeat the design in reverse, omitting the center row.

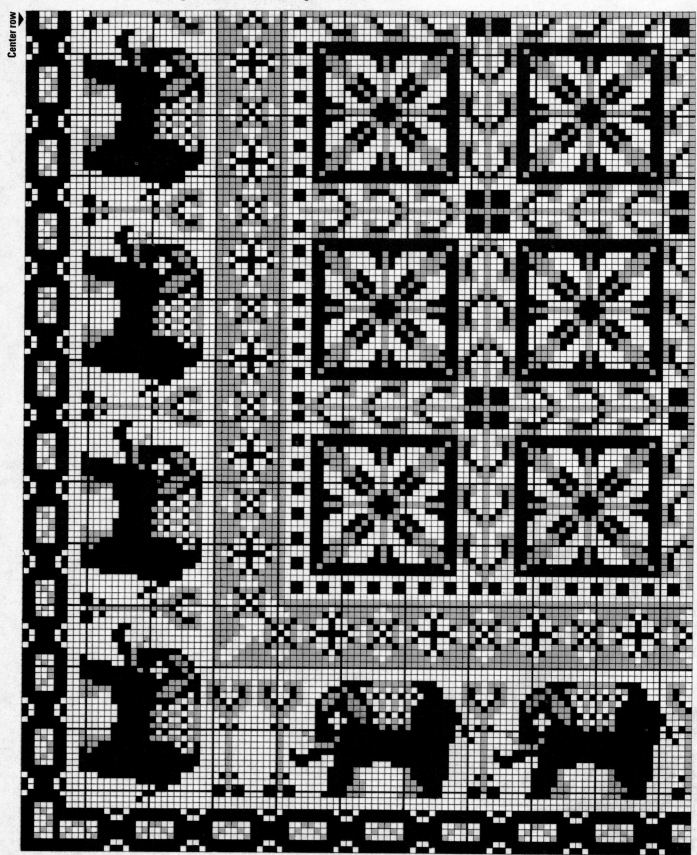

▶ Center row

Center square ▲

Index

Index

Notes

Notes

Notes

Notes